Think Positive for Teens

D0047078

Chicken Soup for the Soul: Think Positive for Teens
Amy Newmark

Published by Chicken Soup for the Soul, LLC www.chickensoup.com
Copyright ©2020 by Chicken Soup for the Soul, LLC. All Rights Reserved.

The publisher gratefully acknowledges the many publishers and individuals who granted Chicken Soup for the Soul permission to reprint the cited material.

Front and back cover images: Torn paper collage courtesy of iStockphoto.com/trinetuzun (©trinetuzun), baseball batter courtesy of iStockphoto.com/YU22(©YU22), guitar courtesy of iStockphoto.com/AlexLMX(©AlexLMX), photo of two girls selfie courtesy of iStockphoto.com/MStudioImages(©MStudioImages), photo of Eiffel Tower courtesy of iStockphoto.com/neirfy (©neirfy), illustration of graduation cap courtesy of iStockphoto.com/saemilee (©saemilee)
Interior pages: photo page 7 courtesy of iStockphoto.com/MStudioImages (©MStudioImages), page 27 illustration courtesy of iStockphoto.com/ Jl19 (©Jly19), page 31 illustration courtesy of iStockphoto.com/Yuliya Derbisheva (©Yuliya Derbisheva), page 37, page 56 photo courtesy of iStockphoto.com/kali9 (©kali9), page 51, page 99 illustration courtesy of iStockphoto.com/mishkom (©mishkom), page 69, page 173 illustration courtesy of iStockphoto.com/elfiny (©elfiny), page 85 illustration courtesy of iStockphoto.com/Asya_mix (©Asya_mix), page 90 photo courtesy of iStockphoto.com/Aiden-Franklin (©Aiden-Franklin), page 115 photo courtesy of iStockphoto.com/Valeriy_G (©Valeriy_G), page 119 illustration courtesy of iStockphoto.com/jammydesign (©jammydesign), page 145 photo courtesy of iStockphoto.com/Kerkez (©Kerkez), page 161 illustration courtesy of iStockphoto.com/ratpack223 (©ratpack223), page 166 photo courtesy of iStockphoto.com/monkey businessimages (©monkeybusinessimages), page 194 photo courtesy of iStockphoto.com/fizkes(©fizkes), page 213 illustration courtesy of iStockphoto.com/kostenkodesign (©kostenkodesign

Photo of Amy Newmark courtesy of Susan Morrow at SwickPix

Cover and Interior by Daniel Zaccari

Distributed to the booktrade by Simon & Schuster. SAN: 200-2442

Publisher's Cataloging-In-Publication Data
(Prepared by The Donohue Group, Inc.)

Names: Newmark, Amy, compiler.
Title: Chicken soup for the soul : think positive for teens / [compiled
    by] Amy Newmark.
Other Titles: Think positive for teens
Description: [Cos Cob, Connecticut] : Chicken Soup for the Soul, LLC, [2020] | Interest age level: 012-017.
    | Summary: "A compilation of personal, revealing stories about teens' real-life experiences that provides a
    roadmap for teens to be the very best they can be. Values such as effort, honesty, respect, self-esteem,
    family bonding, diversity, and volunteering are illustrated by the stories. Some stories are followed by quizzes
    or inspirational quotes that reinforce the lessons learned in the stories"--Provided by publisher.
Identifiers: ISBN 9781611599961 | ISBN 9781611592962 (ebook)
Subjects: LCSH: Teenagers--Conduct of life--Literary collections--Juvenile literature. | Teenagers--Conduct of life--
    Anecdotes--Juvenile literature. | Self-esteem in adolescence--Literary collections--Juvenile literature. | Self-esteem
    in adolescence--Anecdotes--Juvenile literature. | CYAC: Conduct of life--Literary collections. | Conduct of
    life--Anecdotes. | Self-esteem--Literary collections. | Self-esteem--Anecdotes. | LCGFT: Anecdotes.
Classification: LCC BJ1661 .C45 2020 (print) | LCC BJ1661 (ebook) | DDC
    158.10835--dc23

Think Positive for Teens

Amy Newmark

Chicken Soup for the Soul, LLC
Cos Cob, CT

Changing the world one story at a time®
www.chickensoup.com

CONTENTS

❸
DO THE RIGHT THING

❹
MAKE THE EFFORT

❺
FACE YOUR CHALLENGES

❻
COUNT YOUR BLESSINGS

❼
TREASURE YOUR FAMILY

❽
LOOK TO THE FUTURE

INTRODUCTION

Welcome to a new kind of *Chicken Soup for the Soul* book for teenagers. The chapters in this book will help you "think positive" and be the very best, happiest version of yourself.

In Chapter 1, "Be You," you'll be reassured that being yourself really is the best solution. In Brianne Monett's story about copying a popular girl who was "all of the things I thought I wanted to be," she concludes, after an embarrassing eavesdropping incident, "I decided I was going to stop crying and discover who I was." In that same chapter, Fallon Kane overcomes her shyness by taking a job at a store and explains her transformation by saying "Self-esteem is knowing who you are and not being afraid to let it shine."

Have you ever said you needed new friends? In Chapter 2, "Make True Friends," you'll meet some teenagers who found new friends in the most unlikely places. Faith Northmen made a surprising discovery about one of the prettiest, most athletic girls in her class: "I was knocked off balance to realize that, princess though she seemed, she was hurting the same way I was." That led to a new friendship with a truly nice girl who was a lot more like her than Faith had realized.

Sometimes being a friend to someone is not only the right thing to do but the most rewarding also. In Chapter 3, "Do the Right Thing," you'll meet teens who stood up for what was right, and spoke up about ignorance and prejudice. One of my personal heroes is Alexis Streb, who reprimanded a teacher who made fun of the kids on "the short bus." Alexis told off that teacher, politely, and the teacher apologized. Alexis says, "I had spoken the truth and what others in the class were probably thinking."

When you find something challenging you sometimes have to push yourself to try anyway, so in Chapter 4, "Make the Effort," you'll read stories about kids who risked failure, spoke to a misunderstood neighbor, helped a stranger calm a baby, and left it all on the mat in sports. They found the effort always paid off. Christopher Charles McDaniel, for example, grew up in Harlem, and says, "I had no purpose and I was going nowhere." That was until he discovered performing and changed his life forever: "At age seventeen, I signed my first professional contract—with the Dance Theatre of Harlem ensemble." You can check him out on IMDb now!

Being a teenager is tough, so Chapter 5, "Face Your Challenges," is full of inspiration for you, from kids who overcame eating disorders, serious illnesses, parents on drugs, coming out, stuttering, and being that very short kid. Mallory Lavoie tells us that food had become her enemy because "The negative self-talk was crushing me." She eventually concluded, "In cherishing our own flaws, imperfections and uniqueness lies our true beauty."

There are so many studies that prove that gratitude is a proven source of happiness, and that's why we included Chapter 6, "Count Your Blessings." So many kids think the grass is always greener on the other side of the fence, as Diane Stark learned when she spoke to a wealthy friend who seemed to have it all, but really envied Diane's own life with a very involved, affectionate family. She said, "People think I have this great life, but I have struggles too." Tracy Rusiniak went on a church mission trip to help build homes for people who barely had food and shelter, and that caused her to reassess all the things that she thought were so important: "I began to realize how frivolous various aspects of my own life were."

Being grateful for your parents and siblings and grandparents matters, too, even though they sometimes don't seem to get it. In Chapter 7, "Treasure Your Family," Nicole Webster tells us how her volunteer work with a little boy made her realize she had been neglecting her own family. She says, "I had just spent nine months getting to know a kid, but I couldn't say the same thing about my own brother and sister." And Megan Thurlow had her own epiphany when she realized that her father was crushed that he couldn't make it to her championship game because he had to work. She stopped taking it so personally and says, "I began to understand how it must feel to be a father."

One of the hardest parts of being a teenager is that it can feel like you're spending all of middle school preparing for high school, and all of high school preparing for adulthood.

Every decision, every success, and every failure seem incredibly important, so in Chapter 8, "Look to the Future," we put everything in perspective. Tanya Bermudez, for example, thought her bad knee had ruined her future, but learned she had plenty of other ways to succeed, saying, "It turns out that when I lost the chance to play soccer, I found a new future for myself." And Makaila Fenwick shares a cautionary tale about drinking and driving that pertains to all the decisions you have to make as you grow up, saying "Every choice, whether good or bad, is like a pebble dropped into still water."

"A pebble dropped into still water." Here's hoping that every one of these stories makes its own positive impact on your life and that those little waves carry you across the water to adulthood with new tools for handling whatever life throws at you.

—Amy Newmark—
Editor-in-Chief and Publisher
Chicken Soup for the Soul

BE YOU

Finding My Place

Every blade of grass has its angel that
bends over it and whispers, "Grow, grow."
-The Talmud

"Well?" my teacher prompted. "Do you know the answer?" I shifted uneasily in my seat and glanced around the classroom.

Forcing myself to meet her eyes, and in a voice I hoped was nonchalant, I said, "No idea." Not noticing the tears in my eyes, she continued the math lesson. The rest of the day dragged on slowly, until finally the last bell rang. A signal of freedom, until the next day.

A throng of kids flew past me. I felt out of place at school, and I found no comfort with my family either. All the pain, frustration, anger, and embarrassment I had to face in school only intensified at home.

What would my parents, who raised my five older brothers, all budding intellectuals, want to do with a nothing like me? Me, the failure who had to be in a separate class because he couldn't learn? The one who needed to repeat kindergarten when most of his brothers had already skipped a grade.

I always had a tough time in school. My father had put it best: "Some kids are good in school, and some aren't. You're just one of the kids who isn't." But I wasn't satisfied with that answer.

Ever since the first day of school, it had been drilled into my brain that I must strive for academic success. Our principal talked to us many times about striving for greatness. Pictures of past scholars and professors adorned at least one wall of almost every classroom.

I felt I wasn't as good.

But school wasn't the worst of my troubles; my time at home had the greatest effect on me. Whether it was the glowing reports on my brothers, or even the A's and B's on their report cards, I felt I wasn't as good. That I was inferior. (It was only later that I realized I had blown things a bit out of proportion.)

By fourth grade, my self-confidence had shrunk considerably and I became depressed. As I only had a couple of friends, and I wasn't even sure they liked me, I had no one to talk to. I would lie awake at night and wonder if my life had any meaning. Weren't my brothers embarrassed by me? Did they see me as the failure of the family? The black sheep? Tears would soak my pillow. Eventually I would drift off into an uneasy sleep.

I had been tested three years earlier, and they found that I had several learning disabilities. I had to review constantly to keep the information in my brain, and I was always two to three years behind my grade level in math.

As the work became harder, and the shame too much to bear, the depression I had suffered the past two years snowballed into suicidal thoughts. I would wonder, long after I should've been asleep, if life was worth living. Thankfully, I never acted on those thoughts.

Rarely did I accept a compliment on achievements in school or at home, always shrugging it off and telling myself that they didn't really mean it. To make matters worse, my brothers had all gone to the same elementary school. So all the teachers had known them, and

> I was living with the ghosts of their pasts, and I simply couldn't keep up.

I thought I had to keep up the "winning streak." I was living with the ghosts of their pasts, and I simply couldn't keep up.

In high school, without special ed, I had to find new ways to help myself do better in school. But the strain from the past six years had caught up with me, and I loathed working. I had had enough failure in my life. Why add more salt to the wound?

After school one night during my sophomore year, I was working with my tutor. I just wasn't getting it, and it had been going on like that for a few weeks. My tutor had finally had it, and started yelling at me in front of the entire crowd of kids (each with their own private tutor). "How dumb can you be? We've been reviewing the same four math steps for three weeks now. If you don't start shaping up soon, you'll end up being a failure."

That was the first time someone had said "you're a failure" right to my face. Until then, my failure had been my private despair. I stormed out of the room and hid in a dark corner right outside the school. I stayed there for a half hour, crying and asking God if the pain and disappointment would ever end.

I left that school shortly afterwards, hoping to find a place where I could get away from the pain and find the greatness buried deep within me. And I did. My new school has allowed me to see myself in a better light and recognize how much I have grown. The academics aren't as intense as my previous school and I've opened up to others, no longer scared of what they'll think of me. I have built new bonds — not based on academic skill but on true friendship.

I can look in the mirror and see, not what I should be, but what I am. That it doesn't matter who gets the good grades, but rather how I conduct myself and act that matter most. I realized that I had been looking at it all the wrong way — evaluating myself on my abilities, not on my potential to grow into a wonderful person. I had been so wrapped up in the academic side of things that I forgot to look at the person underneath.

> I had been so wrapped up in the academic side of things that I forgot to look at the person underneath.

People greet me cheerfully each morning because they see my inner spark. They see that I'm a friendly and caring person. They don't care if I fail my classes or don't do well on tests. They care about the person, not the achievements. They want to be with me because of who I am as a person. Me! The person who tries as hard as he can in class. The one

who works to make himself into the best person he can be.
This year has breathed new life into me.

— Louis R. Cardona —
Chicken Soup for the Soul: Find Your Inner Strength

Fitting In

If you don't control your mind,
someone else will.
–John Allston

I wasn't the most popular kid my freshman year... not even close. In fact, I was awkward. I wasn't into fashion, preferred reading to sports, had difficulty talking to boys — the whole deal. As a result, the first year of high school had not been kind to me. I had no close friends. I mostly kept to myself with my head buried in a book. Which is why I was so surprised when Ashley and I became friends the summer before sophomore year.

Ashley was very different from me. She was outspoken and fashionable. She listened to bands I had never heard of and was very artistic. She was quite popular and she had been for as long as I could remember. These were qualities I knew nothing about. We had always been in the same classes throughout school, but had never really talked much. I was always intimidated by her.

During summer school, we were both taking classes in

hopes of graduating early. The teacher paired us up on an assignment. Ashley seemed reluctant to work with me at first, but she relented, I imagine, because none of her "cool" friends were in the class. We met at the library to work on the project and really hit it off. Ashley did most of the talking. We sat by each other the rest of the summer and when classes ended we continued to hang out. We went shopping, listened to music, went to movies and to the beach. Everything that you could imagine a great summer with a new friend would consist of.

I looked up to Ashley, idolized her even; she was all of the things I thought I wanted to be. I began listening to the music she listened to, wearing the clothes she wore. I quit reading and started watching the TV programs Ashley watched. I even tailored my sophomore year schedule to her interests. I decided to take art class even though I had really wanted to take theatre. (Ashley found acting dull.) When we started school again, Ashley introduced me to her group of friends, the "cool girls." She was the leader of their group; I would hang out with them on lunch breaks and take classes they were in. I would tag along to football games and I joined art club after school so I could hang out with them even more. Finally I fit in. I followed them around, laughing when they told jokes, agreeing when they had opinions — most enthusiastically at the ones I disagreed with. I didn't say much. I wouldn't want them to think that I was being rude by disagreeing. This continued for several months.

> **She was all of the things I thought I wanted to be.**

One day, I skipped out of my last class a few minutes early so I could get a booth for our group at the diner across from school. This is where we would meet before our Friday afternoon art club. I slouched down in the seat and began working on some homework, awaiting their arrival. Concentrating on my paper, I didn't notice that they had sat down at the booth behind me. Before I could say a word, I realized what they were talking about.

I listened silently. "She's such a loser," one girl said to the group.

"I know, Ashley. She just follows you around trying to be you. She copies you; she doesn't have a personality of her own," another girl added.

> "She copies you; she doesn't have a personality of her own."

Then the Queen Bee herself replied, "I know, I wish she would leave us alone. We were in summer school together and now she thinks we're best friends or something. Get a life."

I was mortified. This was the moment I remember feeling heartbreak for the very first time. My hands were shaking, my face felt hot, and my eyes began to well with uncontrollable tears. How had this happened? I thought we were friends. I didn't know she thought of me in that way. Had I always been a burden to them? I couldn't stay there and listen anymore. I got up and ran out the door. The girls sat in the booth silent as they realized I had heard the whole conversation.

I ran home and told my mother what had happened.

She just held me while I sobbed for hours. I felt so alone and betrayed. I wanted to curl up in my bed and stay there forever, but I knew I would have to go back eventually. The advice my mother gave was so simple. I had heard it a million times, but this time it felt so profound: "Just be yourself and people will like you for who you are." Then and there

> **I decided I was going to stop crying and discover who I was.**

I decided I was going to stop crying and discover who I was. That is exactly what I did.

Ashley and I didn't speak anymore after that. I always thought she felt bad and didn't know how to express it. We would pass in the hall, as if we had never been friends at all. Over the next month, I went through a lot of changes. I bought new clothes, the clothes that I wanted to wear. I dropped art class and joined theatre. I began making new friends who liked me for who I was. I rediscovered reading, and developed my own opinions. I never again just followed the crowd.

I built up the courage to audition for the school play, and actually got a part. I was in every play for the rest of my high school career, landing quite a few lead roles. I had the opportunity to compete at the local and national level, taking many first place ribbons. The friends I made in theatre are still my great friends to this day.

I had an incredible school year. When I look back, I think of it as the year I discovered the person I was going to be. Despite the pain I felt that day, it was a gift they had given me. They opened my eyes. The things that they said about me were true. I was just following, trying desperately to fit in. If I had not been given the chance to realize it, I might have been too concerned with "fitting in" to experience some of the best times of my life.

— Brianne Monett —
Chicken Soup for the Soul: Just for Teenagers

Have you ever tried to be like someone else?

Circle one   YES!   NO!

Name 3 things about you that make you who you are:

1. _____

2. _____

3. _____

Being a Band Babe

We are more than a bunch of nerds.
We can kick butts, too.
—Ryan Jacobson

This story is for all the marching band geeks out there who aren't really geeks. We have friends and lives. We wear make-up and blow-dry our hair. We can hold a conversation without using the words "drill sheets" or "fermata." But we may just happen to play the tuba or the trumpet and start a story or two with "At band camp..." We are regrettably — but proudly — band geeks.

I joined the marching band my sophomore year of high school because I had to. I was no longer doing a fall sport, and my band teacher had made marching band mandatory if you wanted to be in concert band class. I had played the alto saxophone since elementary school.

"Ugh, band camp," I bemoaned to my best friend Natalie, when we both

> We were going to be joining the nerd brigade at the end of the summer.

signed up and realized we were going to be joining the nerd brigade at the end of the summer. We looked at each other and made disgusted faces, deciding we would work to keep each other sane.

As we had expected, band camp sucked. From 8 a.m. to 8 p.m. we were outside in the sweltering sun or the rain for an entire week. We were forced to do push-ups when a trumpet gave some attitude. We had to run laps when the tuba forgot his music. I got a very unflattering tan on my chest from my saxophone neck strap and was sweaty, dirty, and exhausted. I'd come home, collapse on the couch, and pray the next day would be better.

It was a love-hate relationship between the Westhill High School Viking Marching Band and me. Because I played the saxophone, a heavily male-dominated instrument, I was the only girl in my section when I started. The boys were obnoxious and obscene and many of their conversations shouldn't be repeated.

"Yo, that girl what's-her-name in color guard has a nice rack," our section leader would say, literally over my head to his friend.

"Yeah," his friend would laugh. "You know what I'd like to do with her..."

I'd stare at them, trying to remind them with my burning gaze that I was present and not at all amused. Of course,

> By the time I was a junior, I was friends with the whole band.

our section leader disregarded this completely and continued.

But I found that, by the time I was a junior, I was friends with the whole band. I also not-so-secretly enjoyed the attention

I got from my geeky but loveable male bandmates. Natalie and I would wear make-up to band practice and put ribbons on our instruments. I wore my pink pea coat when it got cold out and I fought vainly to feel feminine in the boxy, ugly uniform, waiting as long as I could to put everything on, including the hideous pants with suspenders and drillmaster shoes.

"You look so cute!" my mom would say after she watched a competition. "Just like a little man out there!" I'd then look at her pictures and realize she had taken photographs of someone else, someone who actually was a boy. It was hard to distinguish who was who when we all had on our tall, cylindrical hats with plumes.

I hate to admit it, but marching band was fun. I remember long drives to competitions, on the school bus, with music blasting from a stereo. "We Are the Champions," by Queen, playing and everyone singing along, the bus almost swaying back and forth from our intense jamming.

Competitions would run late and we would sit, fingers crossed, on dark bleachers huddled under blankets, waiting to hear if our name would be called in fourth, third, second, or perhaps even first place. We would scream and hug if the outcome was good, or mope all the way back to the school bus if it was bad. But at least we moped together.

I remember, and sometimes even fondly, the smell of the bus after we'd compete. I'd climb the stairs and be smacked in the face by the vulgar odor of boys' sweat, dirty clothes, and cologne that they thought would make the smell better, but in fact made it almost unbearable. I'd quickly strip down and change — we were all close at this point, and keeping my sweaty band uniform on was way worse than allowing a few teenage boys a glimpse of my bra — and run off the bus, my nose plugged, trying not to gag.

Natalie and I marched our way through three years of band, and by the time we were seniors, we were experts. We showed the freshmen how it was done and proudly put "Section Leader" on our academic

> I find I have a special bond with people who did marching band in high school.

resumes. We loved the band, and the band loved us back. Now that I'm in college, I find I have a special bond with people who did marching band in high school. We speak the same language and understand the band lingo that no one else really does. And, sure, we get looks from people as we start to go off on the subject of drum majors and basics practice. But the people I met in marching band and the things I learned from it greatly outweigh the geek factor — by a lot.

— Madeline Clapps —
Chicken Soup for the Soul: Teens Talk High School

The Bikini

Never violate the sacredness of your
individual self-respect.
—Theodore Parker

ummer was just around the corner and I was going
through a really self-conscious stage. I wanted to wear
a great bikini and look great in it, so I asked my boyfriend Jack to go shopping with me to pick one out.
He was always really helpful, telling me what looked good
and what didn't.

At the mall I picked out several bikinis and retreated to
the changing room. I emerged a few minutes later wearing a
little black bikini. I really liked it.

But Jack wasn't so sure. I could tell by the look on his
face he didn't like it so I tried on several more. But each time I
came out of the changing room he had the same disapproving
look on his face.

"You don't like any of them?" I asked.

He hesitated a moment. "I just think you should lose a
few pounds if you want to wear a bikini."

I was depressed. I felt really fat. I put all the suits back and left without buying any of them. On the drive home Jack had a suggestion for me.

"I bet if you went to the gym and worked out for a few weeks you'd look great in a bikini."

I figured he was right. So the next day I found a gym near my house and walked in, ready to sign up, ready to do anything to look good in a bikini. I wanted Jack to be proud of how I looked when we hung out at the beach.

A really cute guy my age walked up to the front desk. "Can I help you?" He was adorable. I could tell he worked out, but he wasn't too beefy.

"I want to join the gym. I need to lose a few pounds so I can wear a bikini this summer," I explained, a little nervous about telling him why.

> "You should lose a few pounds if you want to wear a bikini."

"You think you need to lose weight to wear a bikini?" he asked, surprised.

"Yeah. My boyfriend thinks if I work out for a few weeks I'll look better."

He just looked at me for a moment, then shook my hand. "I'm Brian."

"I'm Christine."

"Nice to meet you," he said. He smiled at me. I felt a tingle go down my spine.

For the next few weeks I went almost every day to the gym. Brian showed me how to use all the machines. Even though I was feeling more toned and happier about how I looked, I realized something. I wasn't doing it for Jack. And Brian was right. I didn't need to lose any weight.

> I broke up with Jack for making me feel bad about myself.

A funny thing happened during those few weeks. Brian and I became great friends, and when I broke up with Jack for making me feel bad about myself, Brian and I began dating. He never once told me I needed to lose weight. He just supported what I wanted. Most importantly, he liked me just the way I was when I first walked into the gym.

—Christine Dixon—
Chicken Soup for the Soul: Just for Teenagers

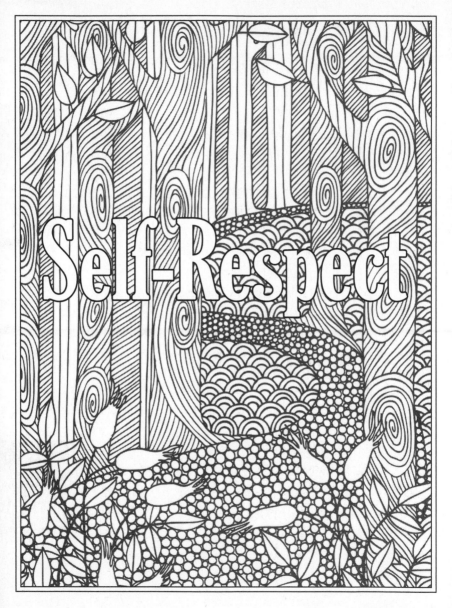

Self-Respect

Pickles

*You yourself, as much as anybody
in the entire universe, deserve your
love and affection.*
~Gautama Buddha

I work in a pickle shop. Okay, we sell things other than pickles — sauces, salsas, and marinades — all packaged in large glass mason jars with matching shiny gold lids. But pickles are what we are known for. When you envision an old-fashioned pickle shop, the stereotypical ideas you might have — food sold in barrels, employees wearing button-downs and jeans and dirty aprons, and a plethora of America-the-great themed décor — are all true. So I just say I work in a pickle shop.

When I was hired, I was told that part of my job was to keep the conversation going with customers. This made me nervous. I had never been a very talkative person. But I fudged the truth on my application and said that I was totally comfortable with talking with strangers.

Fake it till you make it. That's what I did. I sucked it up, put on my button-down, my jeans, my dirty apron, and I entered that pickle shop with a smile on my face. And I decided to just let my real self shine through.

> I decided to just let my real self shine through.

A year and a half later, I am the most tenured employee and have no problem easing into conversations with new customers. I smile, ask them about their day, comment on the great sale. Then I convince them to buy three jars of our pickled garlic.

It is in this pickle store that I learned what self-esteem truly was. Previously, I had always pictured it to be a quality solely possessed by the skinny blond cheerleaders in high school. I am neither skinny, nor blond, and I'm certainly not a cheerleader. While working my way up the ladder at the pickle shop, I worked my way to a broader definition of self-esteem as well.

Self-esteem is knowing who you are and not being afraid to let it shine. My big smile and loud laugh, once a source of embarrassment, has become a sort of trademark for me. It helps me with my sales because customers feel like I am a real person, not just a robotic saleswoman.

Self-esteem is not being completely shut down by a mistake. I once had a customer tell me I was annoying. Pre-pickle shop, I might have crumbled and refused to talk to another customer. Instead, with my new self-confidence, I smiled, apologized, and moved on to the next person, knowing that this woman

> **Self-esteem is knowing who you are and not being afraid to let it shine.**

was the exception, not the rule.

Because of my pickle-shop self-esteem, I applied myself at college. Freshman year I was elected to the boards of two large clubs while maintaining a 4.0 GPA.

It took eighteen years and a store full of pickles to teach me to be happy with myself.

— Fallon Kane —
Chicken Soup for the Soul: Reboot Your Life

Show your
real self
through
your smile

Three Simple Words

*You will never fully believe in yourself if
you keep comparing yourself to everyone
else. Instead, compare yourself
to who you were yesterday.*
~Author Unknown

"Maybe I would be better off if I became an angel tonight," I thought to myself. "I could go to Heaven and watch the show from up there. Then I wouldn't have to be on the stage, and no one would ever call me gimpy or depressed or a burden ever again."

Thinking about hurting myself was the most terrifying thing in the world. I didn't want to die; I just didn't want to feel anymore. But as soon as I thought about the people I loved, I was ashamed for even thinking of doing such a thing. Cerebral palsy

> I just didn't want
> to feel anymore.

didn't have to take over my life. I was lucky mine was extremely mild and something I learned to deal with. My mom and dad raised me with the attitude that I could do anything I set my mind to, regardless of the fact that I spent time in physical therapy. So how did I go from simply walking a little differently to feeling like I could never be good enough because of my limp?

Three months earlier, life could not have been any better. I had been cast in the role I wanted in our upcoming musical. Performing provided me with the greatest rush. I can only describe it as a wonderful mix of feeling like I was simultaneously dreaming and flying. After being a member of the ensemble during previous productions, I was excited that this time around I would have more stage time, including choreography. This was a big accomplishment for any high school performer, but having your talent rewarded while trying to balance a physical challenge, too? That was like the cherry on top.

Our director Anthony was right out of college and one of the hardest working people I knew. His love for theater was always apparent, and it was rare that he was working on fewer than three shows at once. But as busy as he was, he always found the time to give me a hug or reassurance when CP was giving me a rough day. The trust that the two of us shared was unique to any person I had ever worked with. We made a deal from the start. I promised that I would work as hard as my body would let me, and he promised that he would tell me if something looked awkward on stage because of my weak leg. We shook on it, and from then on he never questioned when I asked for a break because my muscles were sore, or if choreography needed to be altered a bit so I could feel comfortable and confident in what I was doing.

> **I eventually became my own worst enemy.**

But as many times as Anthony tried to help me feel secure, I eventually became my own worst enemy, convinced that if I didn't push myself as hard as possible, someone would say that cerebral palsy made me weak and unworthy of being a performer. My insecurities began affecting everything I was doing. I became more and more depressed and felt isolated from the rest of the cast. My usually respectable grades began to drop, which caused even more frustration during what many agree to be the most stressful year of high school — junior year. I left rehearsal each night angry at myself that I had gone from feeling great about earning the part to feeling like I couldn't handle it. Ironically, the motto of our show was "Anything's Possible!" But at the time, it felt like those words couldn't possibly apply to a girl who was stuck in such an overwhelming rut.

Something deep down inside told me I needed to get it together. Not only was our show opening that weekend but previews were happening the next day. The entire school would be coming to watch us perform select scenes from the show. This time around, I was featured in one of the dance numbers, which made me feel incredibly vulnerable. So, after our final dress rehearsal, I found myself standing backstage with Anthony... again. Standing up against the wall in full make-up, I crossed my right leg over my left in an attempt to hide the fact that it was shaking uncontrollably.

"I'm so afraid about tomorrow," I started. "I know I have to get up there and dance but I'm so nervous. What if someone calls me Gimpy again? I don't know if I can handle it. It's killing me!" Everything came flooding out of my mouth so fast that I'm not sure if it made any sense. It was only pure exhaustion that kept me from bursting into tears.

"But Annie," he answered without missing a beat, "why do you care what everyone out there thinks?" His question was so matter-of fact that it startled me, but it made me think. Why did I care so much?

"Listen," he went on, "go out there and forget about what every single person in the audience is thinking. You perform because it is what you love to do. So just go out there and make yourself happy."

Those words rang in my ears for the rest of the night. "Make yourself happy."

His advice was so simple, yet

> **"So just go out there and make yourself happy."**

so powerful. Anthony didn't know about my failing grades, crumbling friendships or the rock bottom I'd hit the night before, but somehow his advice helped me find the power to look at my situation differently. Limp or no limp, I still loved the feeling I had when I was performing. I was glad someone had faith that I could find it again.

The next morning, as I walked into the theater, Anthony looked at me with a smile and said, "Remember what I told you!" While I waited in the wings, I whispered "be happy" to myself and let my mind go blank. The music started. I didn't think, just performed, and I was once again blessed with the joy I thought I had lost. I consider that afternoon to be one of my happiest moments. Not because of some huge epiphany or raving audience, but because my heart felt ten pounds lighter as I walked off the stage.

I'm not sure either of us realized it at the time, but my director's words to me as a high school girl changed me and will always stay close to my heart. I have not only remembered them... I've lived by them. My CP will never go away, but I know that it's a blessing in disguise, made even more valuable because of my experiences in theater. Every day I am grateful for the journey that helped me become a better, more positive person. One that began because of three simple words: make yourself happy.

— Annie Nason —
Chicken Soup for the Soul: Think Possible

Chapter 2

MAKE TRUE FRIENDS

Chicken Soup for the Soul

What Is Wrong with You?

The antidote for fifty enemies
is one friend.
~Aristotle

"Isn't your cross supposed to be upside down?" The freshman boy looked at me with eyebrows raised too innocently, while his friends behind him snickered and did a poor job of hiding their laughter. I gripped my lunch tightly, helplessly aware that there were no more places to sit, no holes to squeeze myself into and just disappear... forever.

"Why would my cross be upside down?" I asked, rolling my eyes. I was tired of this and finally starting to get angry.

Delighted in the attention he was getting from his inquiry, he gestured to me, "Aren't you Gothic?"

I couldn't answer. My tongue was classically stuck to the roof of my mouth.

"Um, hello... what is wrong with you?"

I coughed out a quick, "Yeah, right," and walked away.

It's already difficult being a freshman. It's impossible being a Goth freshman at a Christian school. All the teachers know your name. You're at the top of an intervention list. I didn't make much noise but I could silence a room instantly and clear a lunch table in less than thirty seconds. Routinely I was sent to the principal's office: Was I struggling in my spiritual life? Had I ever dabbled in witchcraft? Why did I want to look like that? Was someone hurting me? Was I hurting someone?

However, the reason I wore black was actually very boring: I liked black and I liked old-fashioned dresses. Today we call it "steampunk" and it has a more positive, trendy association, but to everyone at my school it was considered nothing short of walking with the Devil. I hadn't really wanted to fit in or be popular, but I had wanted to be accepted and somewhat liked. Before long, I realized that only the beautiful people made the grade, figuratively and literally. There seemed to be an entirely different set of rules for the prettiest, most athletic girls. Honestly, I didn't mind them doing their thing — why couldn't they just let me do mine?

> There seemed to be an entirely different set of rules for the prettiest, most athletic girls.

I dreaded going to bed at night, because going to bed at night meant waking up in the morning and going to school. As we pulled into the parking lot every morning, my chest would tighten painfully and my pulse would start to race. Walking through the gate, I would cringe and ignore the urge to cry.

With each disapproving stare from teachers and sneer from "good students," I tried not to cover my face and run from the building. It wasn't long before I started asking myself: *What is wrong with me?*

Then, when it seemed like things were already too hurtful to bear, a growing pain in my lower abdomen began matching my emotional pain. I often left class for the restroom, where I lay on the cool floor and cried from a deep, lacerating clawing in the middle of my body.

One night, I was carried into the emergency room with crippling pain. Over the next few weeks, I was given a series of tests, hormone therapy, and medication. The doctors diagnosed me with endometriosis and a broken cyst. I probably wouldn't be able to have kids, and in the future a hysterectomy might be necessary. There was no cure.

Back in school, I was limited to walking the track during P.E., and I was actually thankful for the seclusion. However, like bloodhounds, high school girls smell fear and pain. The popular girls jumped on another girl while I was separated from them.

"So, what's wrong with you?" they asked her.

She was slender and delicate, blond with fair skin and pretty hazel eyes. I disliked her on principle because she looked like a Disney princess. She wore pinks and pastels, short skirts and girly sandals, and her make-up always seemed perfect. In junior high, she struggled with her weight. Now she was trim, elegant, a content resident of the popular table. Her name was Missy, and as far as I was concerned, she was one of them.

While I laced up my shoes, I heard Missy explain to the other girls that she had been absent due to a flair-up of lupus. Two of the girls jumped back immediately, thinking lupus was contagious. The other two went on about how lucky she was to get to walk instead of play sports.

Lucky? I mean, really? Disgusted, I turned around and started walking. Instead of the seclusion I had hoped for, quiet little Miss Cinderella joined me around the track.

I watched her cautiously from the corner of my eye. The safe thing would be to say as little as possible. Gradually, however, Missy and I began to chat. I was surprised when I didn't have to explain words like "endometriosis" and "broken cyst" to her. She understood the havoc hormone therapy was having on my emotional life and she didn't respond with false cheerfulness or the other extreme: horror. In a strange twist of fate, Missy and I found ourselves comforting and understanding each other. I knew how we looked together, me with my combat boots, occasional trench coat, corset, and long skirts, and Missy with her summery blouses and trendy slippers. We just did not belong. I was knocked off balance to realize that, princess though she seemed, she was hurting the same way I was.

> I was knocked off balance to realize that, princess though she seemed, she was hurting the same way I was.

As I got to know Missy, I realized people were talking about her almost as much as they were talking about me. Her popularity had come with a high price, one she didn't choose to pay. When her doctor switched her medicines between eighth and ninth grade, she lost her childhood baby fat and got her elegant adult figure, because she was constantly sick to her stomach.

Once Missy and I became visible friends, a sharp line was drawn between her and her old friends. Sure enough, she started hanging out with me less and less, and for a short time not at all. But then she did come back, arriving late to lunch, looking like she'd been hassled.

Missy and I became best friends, and years later, we're still best friends. In fact, under the protection of our friendship, I've been known to wear pink lace and she's been known to wear black boots. It was some time later I learned why Missy had come to lunch late, looking exhausted and uncomfortable. In a style that would have made the Spanish Inquisition proud, Missy had been set upon by her old "friends" and interrogated... about me.

Is she a witch?

Is she demon possessed?

Is she insane?

Does she worship Satan?

It had been a perfect chance for Missy to secure her position at the top of the ninth grade social food chain. Instead, she cast her lot with me — social suicide. She just told those girls that I liked black and there was nothing wrong with me.

— Faith Northmen —
Chicken Soup for the Soul: Just for Teenagers

Have you ever been teased for being different? What is your action plan?

☐ Tell my friends not to tease people for being different.

☐ Reach out to someone who is being teased, and help.

☐ Find friends who accept differences.

☐ Don't be afraid to show my own differences.

Best Friends

Somewhere on this planet is your
best friend. Find that person.
-Omar Kiam

My best friend knows me well,
And reads me like a book.
She knows when there is something wrong
By taking just one look.

She also reads between the lines,
When I've got things to share.
She listens without judging me
And lets me know she cares.

She tells me what I need to hear,
I know it's for my good.
Otherwise, I'd never change
Or do the things I should.

She laughs when I am happy,
And cries when I am hurt.
She stands firm and takes my side
When others dish out dirt.

Our friendship is forever,
It's priceless and won't end.
I'm absolutely sure of this
'Cause I'm also her best friend.

— Lydia Gomez Reyes —
Chicken Soup for the Soul: Just Us Girls

From Hare to Tortoise

Success is blocked by concentrating on it and planning for it.... Success is shy—it won't come out while you're watching.
—Tennessee Williams

I entered my freshman year of high school with a definite philosophy: work hard and stick to whatever I could succeed at. In this way, I reasoned, I'd be able to skate through high school and out the other side with a 4.0 and some impressive accomplishments. I wouldn't waste my time in areas where I didn't excel.

And this philosophy served me well. I worked hard in my classes and on cello practice and got the results I wanted, usually in the shape of grades, successful recitals, and other materialistic rewards. My academic standards were high, because my dreams for the future were ambitious. An A- would've been the end of the world. My friends would tease me about my all-or-nothing attitude, but in my eyes, it was the only sure path to success.

At the beginning of sophomore year, I fully intended to keep that same attitude. Then I joined the cross-country running team, a year after I'd watched cross-country races and said, "I could never do that!" I joined mainly because my brother was on the team; he was entering his senior year, and I wanted to spend as much time with him as possible before he left for college. Also, most of my friends were on the team, and they'd been trying to cajole me into running for months. When I came to the first practice, I was filled with optimism and grandiose dreams of making the varsity team.

But as the distance we ran each practice gradually increased from three, to four, to six miles, I realized with surprise that no matter how hard I tried, I wasn't physically capable of running as **I wasn't physically capable of running as fast as my friends.** fast as my friends. I wouldn't be on varsity; in fact, I was one of the slowest on the team. This concept eroded my dream of running prowess. And the muscular strain of cross-country was often unbearable, especially on the last scorching and humid days of summer. With every step I ran, my mind reined me in with an endless string of complaints. Not only did I suck at running, but I was having no fun! What was the point of putting myself through so much pain? I'd never make points for U-32 in a race; I'd just be letting down my team. After the first few weeks, I wanted to quit.

Then we had our first cross-country meet. When we got off the bus at Lamoille High School, decked out in our blue uniforms with our team name emblazoned on the jerseys, the sight of the other teams warming up made me cringe. I wasn't the only one; our whole team was wired with nervous anticipation. We jogged to the starting line and went through our warm-ups silently. When we started the race, I felt the enormous pressure of expectations sink onto my shoulders. I watched the churning tide of runners begin to surge past me and was overwhelmed with frustration. It was a brutal course, comprised of a series of short, steep hills that looped around twice, and after a while I stopped running and struggled to walk up the last mammoth hill.

But then I heard my coaches yelling my name from the top of the hill, their cries of encouragement mingling with those of my teammates. I felt confused and embarrassed; why were they cheering for me? I was running terribly!

> I began to put my effort into supporting my teammates instead of obsessing about my own performance.

As I broke into a weary jog up the last stretch of hill, I realized that my coaches didn't care how fast I ran. Neither did my teammates. During the rest of the season, they were always on the sidelines of every race, cheering for me just as loudly as they'd cheered for the frontrunner. Those expectations that had weighed on me so heavily at the beginning of the race were simply my own. And once I realized that, I decided to cast them away. I began to put my effort into supporting my teammates instead of obsessing about my own performance. In that way, I celebrated my teammates' victories as if they were my own; I felt their pain and exhaustion as if they were my own. After a while, it didn't matter if the runners struggling up the hill were on my team or not — I rooted for them anyway. And they would always return the favor whenever I needed it most, because we were linked by the understanding of having been in the same position.

The relationships forged within our cross-country team are ones that will carry on past our running days and into old age. The comradeship of sharing the intense emotions that sprung out of a grueling sport made the bonds between my teammates and me surpass friendship. And often, the emotions we shared were frustration, pain, disappointment, and sheer exhaustion. But together, as a team, we were able to push through those moments together and come out as champions — not as champions of ribbons or trophies, but as champions of perseverance. The memories that stand out most clearly aren't the bitter ones; they're the moments when a teammate loses his shoes in the bog, keeps running barefoot, and laughs about it at the finish line. They're the expressions of pride on my coaches' faces when I tell them I didn't walk once during a whole race. They're the subconscious grins that spread over the runners' faces when they hear us yelling ridiculous things from the sidelines, and the frenzied jumping-up-and-down

> I don't need to be the best to be successful in life.

finish line moments when a teammate breaks his previous best time by two minutes.

To be honest? I don't remember the exact grade I got on my U.S. History summer assignment. When I got my first A- at the end of sophomore year, the world managed to keep turning. Cross-country running made me realize that I don't need to be the best to be successful in life. It taught me to value my relationships with people more than my relationship with my ego. It taught me to cheer for others even if I never learn their first names. High school doesn't last forever. But maybe someday, way down the road, an old high school friend will call me out of the blue. We'll gradually ease back into the familiar with summer memories we shared and jokes we used to laugh at. Maybe we'll stretch our memories all the way back to the days when we were limber enough to run three miles, and she'll say with a laugh, "Do you remember that State Championships meet when there was that downpour and Zac lost his shoes in the bog...?"

And I will.

— Juliette Rose Wunrow —
Chicken Soup for the Soul: Just for Teenagers

Feeling Full

Recovery is remembering who you are and using your strengths to become all that you were meant to be.
~Recovery Innovations

A nxious, obsessive compulsive, and anorexic — had you asked me months ago, I would have told you I was all three. I don't know why then it came as such a shock when the doctor stated I wouldn't be leaving the hospital that morning.

I recognized that I had a problem. But when a medical professional looked at me and said, "You're an anorexic. Your heart, in fact your whole body, is going into failure. You could die," it all suddenly became very real. That diagnosis meant that I couldn't run from it anymore.

I had admitted to my parents that I was suffering from an eating disorder towards the end of tenth grade. What had started as a desire to improve my health rapidly snowballed into a drastically unhealthy change in habits and alarming weight loss. I limited my caloric intake to about 800 calories a day and exercised up to four hours a day. I was consumed with thoughts about my body and how to maintain the "perfect" and completely unattainable goal I had in my mind.

All of this left me with intense emotional distress, physical damage, and a 101-pound devastated body. I had withdrawn and discon-

> **I felt completely hollow and starved of everything in life.**

nected from my social life. I felt completely hollow and starved of everything in life. I was dying, inside and out.

At the beginning of the summer, after having told the truth about my struggle, my parents immediately did all that they could to help. Sadly, the reality of the matter was that help would be months away. I was put on a waiting list for an eating disorders recovery program, so we were left to face my anorexia as best as we could on our own. Though I still failed to consume an appropriate amount, I did will myself to eat more. And although the constant thoughts of exercise prevented me from concentrating, I did cut my workouts in half. Summer was an uphill battle, but come the end of July, my saving grace was just around the corner.

Camp Kintail was a Presbyterian summer camp near Goderich, Ontario, right off Lake Huron, and also known as my home away from home. That summer was my fifth year at camp, and one of my most profound. Kintail had always been my sanctuary. It was the one place that I could truly be my open and honest self. Every summer, I was graced with beautiful people, scenery, and opportunities to grow as an individual.

As a result, I learned that no matter what life threw at me, I could be sure that my time at Kintail could get me through it. That summer I was to spend a month in their leadership program, which ultimately saved my life.

It was my intent to reveal my issue once I got to camp. However, that proved more difficult than I had anticipated. While I had many friends at camp, I felt we'd grown apart. Though I tried, I couldn't bring myself to share my problem. Three days passed and I hadn't told a soul. Then one morning in the lodge, for no reason other than a gut feeling, I approached one of my fellow leaders in training. I knew little more than her name.

"Hayley, can I talk to you?"

Within minutes, tears were pouring down my face as I choked out the truth. To my surprise, she began crying too. She patiently listened to me as I expressed how I felt, but she already knew. When I finished, she looked me in the eyes and said, "One year ago, I was exactly where you are now." Hayley explained that she had overcome her eating disorder the prior summer and firmly believed camp had saved her life. I honestly believe in that very moment she saved mine.

For the rest of camp, Hayley was like my guardian angel. No matter how stressful things got or how difficult I became, she did everything in her power to keep me happy, safe, eating, and feeling supported.

Going home was the hard part, because it meant tests and evaluations, and then waiting until late October for my meeting for the recovery program. But on the third day of school, my stepmom told me that my evaluation had been bumped up. "They saw the result of your preliminary ECG, and they're concerned. They want to see you tomorrow."

With this urgent evaluation came the possibility of admittance into the hospital. It's funny how the world works, because that morning, Hayley (whom I hadn't talked to since camp) contacted me and asked how I was doing. I told her the truth, and she did the same with me. "This is when you have to get better. You're slowly committing suicide. Think about how much you have ahead of you." I honoured her words.

I went to my appointment that morning wearing my kilt and collared top, my hair done, my make-up on. I thought I would be going to school that afternoon. But there I was, sitting in that box of a room, the doctor's words still ringing in my ears. I would not go home for a month.

For quite some time, I blamed myself for this — for the inability to just eat a piece of cake or skip a run. People had reacted strongly upon discovering my illness: "I thought you were smarter than that" and "You've just got to eat." These responses only furthered my self-hatred, and I believed them. Until I started hearing the response from people uncovering the truth: "It's a disease."

It took a lot for me to finally understand that it is a disease. Lying in my hospital bed, devastated and sobbing, I recalled apologizing to my parents for all of the stress I had caused and that I couldn't just be better. They would have none of that. "Would you just tell a cancer patient to get better?" No, I suppose you

"It's a disease."

wouldn't. Thinking that over, I finally accepted that I was sick, and not by my doing. However, getting better would be through my own doing.

My month in that hospital was hands down the hardest month of my life, but I got through it. And I still continue to recover from my disorder. Some days I feel unstoppable, and some days I feel stopped dead in my tracks. Each day, however, I continue to heal and recover, because I have an infinite will to do so.

"I eat. I'm still anorexic."

A friend recovering from her disorder once told me that. It's a statement that explains a lot and holds much truth. I eat, but I still struggle. I'm still ill, and I'm still a long way from being completely better, but that's okay.

It's okay because I have people like Hayley in my life, an incredibly supportive and understanding family, places like Kintail, and a strong drive to recover.

With all of that in mind, I know I'm finally on my way to feeling full again.

— Samantha Molinaro —
Chicken Soup for the Soul: Find Your Inner Strength

The True Meaning of Friendship

*A friend is one of the nicest things
you can have, and one of the
best things you can be.*
—Douglas Pagels

I couldn't believe that I was here again, starting a new chapter in my life. It had only been three years since I was in the same situation. But those doors were much smaller and so was the depth of my knowledge. I heard a ring and in I went. It was time to face it — the first day of high school.

Compared to all the upperclassmen around me, I felt very small. It was honestly the hardest day of my life, and just trying to make it to class on time was difficult. I couldn't believe that so many people knocked over others to get to lunch. What happened to waiting in line? Looking for a lunch table was also tough. High school wasn't like middle school. It was much bigger and harder to make myself stand out. I was used to the attention and to people saying "Hi" in the hallways. Now all I heard was, "Move Freshie!"

The next week was better because at least I knew my locker combination. I hadn't gotten knocked over in the hallways and my schedule was coinciding with my friends'. All I saw around me was happiness — the seniors catching up with each other and bragging about new loves and new adventures. And then I saw her. The prettiest girl I had ever seen: Emily Butler.

Besides the fact that she was ranked number two in her class, took part in numerous activities, was the prettiest and most popular girl in school and a teacher's favorite, and already had a full scholarship to the college of her choice, she had class. She was a role model to everyone and wasn't afraid to tell it like it was. She was so lucky to be so amazing — I could only pray to come that close.

> **She was a role model to everyone.**

As she bumped me in the hallway, she smiled and apologized. Following her were numerous boys and girls. Her laugh could be heard for miles and her teeth were brighter than a cheerleader's positive attitude. I told myself that if I tried really hard, one day I could be just like her. She couldn't have always been perfect, right?

As weeks went on, I joined plenty of activities and got myself involved in numerous sports and volunteer programs. One club I stumbled my way into was Mock Trial. The captain, of course, was glamorous Emily Butler. She instructed and ran the meetings and was very nice to me. As time went on, we became close and she taught me a lot. She always hung out with me and put in the extra mile for me. It was weird, but she treated me like a little sister. The more we hung out, the closer I was to the seniors. I went to parties with them and even hung out one-on-one with them. I became more outgoing and well-liked.

> **It was weird, but she treated me like a little sister.**

In December, I became quite ill with mononucleosis and couldn't go to school for a month. After that, Emily and I stopped hanging out and again I felt alone. Then one day, she called me and asked me to chill with her. I gladly accepted. We began hanging out every day and I was more attached to her than I was to my own boyfriend. She lifted me up and again I became comfortable in my own skin. Each day, I found something more to love about her and myself.

When I would do something wrong, Emily would be there to pick up after my mistakes. When the year finally came to a close, we cried as we said goodbye. She had made my freshman year more than I could have ever hoped for. She said good luck and told me that I was beautiful and had a heart full of love. She told me that if I ever needed her, she would be there for me. She hugged me goodbye and left. Tears rolled down my face and I began to wonder how I could ever survive without her.

As my sophomore year began, I no longer heard people talking about Emily and how great she was, and I missed her loud laugh. We still keep in touch and I hope to become just like her one day. I have already vowed that I, too, will find a freshman to teach and treat like a little sister. Emily taught me that I can do whatever I want, and I will pass on her sweet lesson. She showed me the true meaning of friendship, love, and the courage to be myself.

—Amber Curtis—
Chicken Soup for the Soul: Teens Talk High School

Leave the Door Open

The better part of one's life consists of his friendships.
–Abraham Lincoln

Watching my parents walk to their car after helping me move into my dorm room, I was already feeling homesick. Most people don't leave home and go away for school at the age of fourteen, but there I was, out in the parking lot, waving goodbye to my mom and dad as tears started flowing down my cheeks.

My mom stopped and rushed over to give me one more hug, but she and I both knew there wasn't anything more she could do for me. It was too late to change my mind and go to my local high school closer to home. Too late to gather up all my things and jump into the comfort of my parents' car (and arms). It had been my decision to go to this school that my dad had once attended, and there was no turning back.

Boarding school is often thought of either as a place for

delinquent children or an expensive, preppy, all-girls or all-boys school akin to *The Facts of Life* television show. My high school was called a prep school, but it provided nothing like Blair, Natalie, Tootie and Jo's experience. It was a small religious school. We didn't wear uniforms and while my dormitory floor was all-girls, the school was co-ed. We also had a much younger version of Mrs. Garrett.

I quickly walked back into my dorm room, making sure all my tears were dried first. While fourteen years old is young enough to need a mom's shoulder to cry on, it's definitely too old to let anyone witness it.

> **I longed to be included but was too shy to go into the hall and mingle.**

My roommate wasn't in our room at the time. Earlier I had seen her with a group of girls already fitting in and making friends, whereas I was very quiet and didn't know a soul. I couldn't imagine going up to a group of girls and asking if I could join them. The excitement that filled the air on move-in day only meant heartache for me, as I longed to be included but was too shy to go into the hall and mingle.

Having no clue what I was supposed to do next, I felt alone on a floor filled with freshman girls. I pulled out my desk chair and sat down. Grabbing a pen and paper, I really had no intention of writing anything, but I honestly couldn't think of anything else to do.

Feeling the tears about to make an unwelcome appearance

again, I was glad my desk faced the wall — gray and bleak though it was. I could hear giggling girls trotting back and forth down the hall past my room. It took all my might not to close the door, knowing that doing so would eliminate all chances of making a friend.

Just then two heads peeked into my doorway — my roommate, Becky, followed by a bubbly girl named Holly who said, "All the girls are going downstairs into the Student Union. Want to come?" I sprang up faster than I thought physically possible. Feeling an overwhelming sense of relief, I said, "Sure," and quickly joined my new friends. As Holly, Becky, and I walked down the hall, recruiting more girls to head to the basement lounge with us, I immediately knew I was going to be okay. Maybe more than okay.

For four hours I found myself talking and listening, telling stories

> Growing up together, we became a family.

and laughing with this group that had expanded to about twenty-five girls and boys. We were embarking on a four-year journey together that would equal what most people first experience in their college years. Not only did we share rooms, bathrooms, and three meals a day, we also shared clothes, shoes, late night talks, and the occasional fun of sneaking out after "lights out."

Living together beginning at age fourteen made us quickly become more than just new friends. Growing up together, we became a family. I'm eagerly anticipating a family reunion of sorts this summer at our twenty-year high school reunion. My "new" friends have since become my old friends and without a doubt will remain my forever girlfriends.

— Deanne Haines —
Chicken Soup for the Soul: Just Us Girls

DO THE RIGHT THING

Go to Them

No act of kindness, no matter
how small, is ever wasted.
~Aesop

reshman year of high school, I was new in town, and I knew no one. One of the first friends I made asked me to the homecoming dance. Brian was a model kid — polite, kind and quiet. One very sad day, a year or so into our friendship, Brian's dad passed away unexpectedly. I had not met his dad, but it didn't stop me from feeling heartbroken for my friend. When I told my mom about it, she asked when the service was so we could go.

"What?" I said. "I never knew him. I shouldn't be there."

I was sure that Brian would think my attendance was weird or offensive. Being young and (thankfully) having little experience with death personally, I thought it would be grossly inappropriate for me to show up having not known his dad. Despite the fact that I wished I could do something to show Brian I was sad for him and be there for him, going didn't feel like an option. I felt frozen, upset and unsure of what to do.

Mom explained that such services are not just about the person who's passed away, but so much more about the people left behind. She said it makes a difference just to show up for people, to take time to be with them in their darkest hours. Her words seemed to make sense, but I was still wary that I could make any kind of difference. Reluctantly, I agreed to go.

> **I thought it would be grossly inappropriate for me to show up having not known his dad.**

I was so nervous walking toward the building. I felt I had nothing to offer, even though Mom had told me otherwise. It felt all wrong, like I was trespassing into the most sacred "family and friends only" space for Brian's dad. However, Mom was totally natural — sad, but relaxed and confident in her stride. The steady *click, click, click* of her heels on the pavement kept me steady enough to not run back to the car.

We didn't do anything extraordinary that day. We didn't have fond memories to share with Brian. We didn't make food or even take flowers. We were just there. And, somehow, that was enough. Watching my mom hug Brian made all her words come alive. Then, when I felt the warmth of his hug, it was rewarding for me to share that space, to be so close and convey my pain at his pain, even though I couldn't fix it or take it away. Brian thanked us for being there, and it was clear that he was touched by our presence. I wouldn't and couldn't have gone without Mom encouraging me and teaching me that day

> **If friends are grieving, go to them.**

about compassion.

The lesson I learned that day has always stayed with me: If friends are grieving, go to them. My mom was there to guide me for so many moments like these, when people were grieving, or sick, or needed a safe place. It came so naturally to her; her life's work was being a nurse, after all. She used to say that compassion could be taught, and in her field, it *should* be taught. It was a fascinating concept to me. Little did I realize that she was in the midst of teaching it to me! Mom was right. You *can* teach compassion. She taught me, and I'm sure many others along the way. For that, I thank her.

— Lisa Solorzano Petit —
Chicken Soup for the Soul: Mom Knows Best

The Boldest Girl in Class

Courage is what it takes to stand up and speak; courage is also what it takes to sit down and listen.
~Winston Churchill

I'll never forget the first time I heard my English teacher, Mr. Barnes, make an inappropriate comment in class. He'd just handed out our first assignment and someone asked how long it should be. "Like the length of a lady's skirt," he said. "Long enough to cover everything, but short enough to keep it interesting." The guys howled and gave each other high fives. Mr. Barnes just sat there and smiled with an annoying little smirk on his face. It made my skin crawl.

As the year went by, his comments became more and more inappropriate. I began to dread his class. He could turn anything we studied into something negative and degrading to women. It was humiliating. How could he treat us like this?

Each time he made one of his comments, I wanted to say something, but I was too afraid of him. Besides, everyone called me "Miss Quiet and Shy." I didn't like speaking in front of other people and I would never talk back to a teacher.

Toward the end of the year, we started studying *The Canterbury Tales*, a Middle English collection of stories about a group of travelers. Mr. Barnes made a generic, stereotypical comment about the traveler in each tale we were reading. When we came to the tale about the "Wife of Bath," I braced myself. Just as I suspected, he told us about how this woman was a typical wife. They only brought her along because they needed someone to cook and clean. I just couldn't take it anymore. What was wrong with us? Why did we all sit complacently, taking this abuse? The guys were laughing and acting like Mr. Barnes was a stand-up comedian. I looked at the girls and most of them just sat there with their arms crossed and their heads hanging down. It made me so angry. I felt like I was going to explode.

I don't know what came over me. Suddenly, I blurted out a "Hmm!" My teacher's head jerked up.

He glared around the room and asked, "Who said that?" No one said a word. It was so quiet that I heard the clock on the wall ticking for the first time ever.

I had a queasy feeling in the pit of my stomach, like I'd

> Each time he made one of his comments, I wanted to say something, but I was too afraid of him.

just gone upside down on a roller coaster. I could feel my face getting hotter as the blood rushed to my cheeks. My heart was pounding so loud and so fast that I thought it might jump right out of my chest. What was I thinking? I was "Miss Quiet and Shy," right? I was already in way over my head. Oh well, I thought, somebody has to stand up to this guy — here goes nothing. I opened my mouth and blurted out, "I said it." Everyone whipped around and stared at me with looks of horror. I wanted to crawl underneath my desk.

Mr. Barnes glared at me and said, "Do you have something you'd like to say?"

"Yes... I... do." I choked out. "I think your comments are stereotypical and rude. They are... um... inappropriate, sir." I stammered.

"Well," he said, "I'm sorry you feel that way. Thank you for your comments, Miss Westbrook."

I don't think I paid attention to anything else the entire class period. I couldn't believe what I had just done. Was that my voice I had heard? Did Mr. Barnes really just thank me for my comments? When the bell rang, I grabbed my stuff and ran down the hall to my locker.

> People I didn't even know were coming up to me and patting me on the back.

By the end of the day, the entire school had heard what had happened. People I didn't even know were coming up to me and patting me on the back. All of the girls were so glad that someone had finally stood up to him, and so was I. I just couldn't believe that it had been me!

For the rest of the year, Mr. Barnes toned down his comments, at least in my class. He still told some awful jokes, but they were no longer degrading.

When I handed in my final exam, Mr. Barnes looked me in the eye and said, "You, Miss Westbrook, will go far in life. We need more leaders and fewer followers. Good luck next year." I was shocked — it seemed like he actually respected me for standing up to him. I smiled and felt proud. Who would have thought that "Miss Quiet and Shy" would have ended up being the boldest girl in class?

— Christy Westbrook —
Chicken Soup for the Soul: Teens Talk High School

The Help I Could Give

Dare to reach out your hand into the darkness,
to pull another hand into the light.
~Norman B. Rice

One morning, my best friend comes to me before homeroom and says she needs to tell me something—and show me something. She starts explaining before she even tells me what happened, saying she doesn't know why and doesn't know what to do and she needs my help. She pulls up her shirtsleeve and peels back a Band-Aid. I don't understand at first, but as the world around me slows, all I can focus on is the fact that my best friend, who has always been so strong, is hurting herself. She asks me not to tell anyone, just to help her. She asks me to promise I won't tell and promise I'll help her. I think I can fix her.

We go to her house after school that day and come up with

a plan. We will spend as much time together as possible, and anytime she feels the need to cut she will call me. Everything will be okay. Everything will be all right.

A day or two later, she admits to doing it again. She says she really wants to stop but she doesn't know how. She doesn't know what is wrong with her. I tell her we need to tell someone else, find someone to help, even

> She says she really wants to stop but she doesn't know how.

though all I really want to do is fix her by myself. She tells me no, don't tell anyone yet, and that she doesn't want her parents to know. She doesn't want to let them or her sisters down. I tell her we can wait, and if it happens again, we will tell someone. She agrees, promises we'll stick to the plan this time, and everything will be okay.

It happens again, and then again. I can't concentrate on work. I can't concentrate on school. I can't even begin to think about anything but finding a way to help her. It finally hits me one day in first period. I cannot do this myself. As much as it hurts me to not be able to help her myself, I realize that she needs help I can't give. I find a teacher I trust, my health teacher, and tell her about what is going on. I don't tell her my friend's name yet because I am scared about what will happen next. The morning is a blur of tears and explanations as I am brought to the guidance counselor to figure out the next step. We decide that I will go find my friend and try to convince her to come with me and talk.

I know my friend is in study hall during third period. I

> **I find a teacher I trust, my health teacher, and tell her about what is going on.**

stand outside her class and get her attention — she gets the hall pass and comes out to meet me. I begin to break down. I tell her I can't help her. I can't do it, and I know she needs help that I can't give. I can support her, I can stand by her, but I can't do everything. Finally, she agrees with me. We walk to the guidance office and sit with our guidance counselor, discussing what to do next. We take a walk to the nurse's office to make sure nothing is infected, and for the nurse's guidance, since she has seen wounds like this before. In a strange way, it is comforting to know we are not the only ones to have dealt with this, to know that there are people that can help.

That was the day the slow healing process began. Months after, we were still working towards being okay and learning how to deal. But the beginning was the hardest part. I had to admit that I couldn't just fix my friend and she needed to admit that she needed help helping herself. This problem is something that will keep us close forever. And I realized that day that even though I didn't fix her myself, I was helping her by getting the outside help she needed. We learned how to face what came at us, and now we both know that we are strong. We know that we can get through anything, and that during times when we need it, it is more than okay to ask for help.

— Aimee McCarron —
Chicken Soup for the Soul: Teens Talk High School

Have you ever been afraid to help someone, or you didn't know how? Aimee's friend wanted her to tell someone, but she didn't ask outright.

Who could you tell if a friend was having issues?

1.

2.

3.

Breaking Boundaries

*The time is always right
to do what is right.*
~Dr. Martin Luther King, Jr.

"**N**othing said in this room will leave this room. We are a family tonight, and this is an unbreakable circle of trust."

I laid my head down on my pillow and squeezed my stuffed animal closer to my chest, preparing for the pain and tears I knew were to come. I was going to spend the next few hours of the five-day leadership camp in an activity called Boundary Breaking, during which I would discover the dreams, fears, secrets and struggles of eighteen other high school students, all of whom I had known for a total of two and a half days. I would be expected to completely open myself up to these people, a thought that made me squirm with discomfort.

The questions started off easy, more like icebreakers than the deeply personal questions I was expecting. Yet with each question, I could sense my connection with the members of the group growing, and together we could feel the atmosphere in the room changing. As the intensity of our new relationship increased,

> **I would be expected to completely open myself up to these people.**

so did the intensity in which we responded to the progressively more intimate questioning. Questions such as "What do you fear most?" and "What has been the most difficult time in your life?" began to draw tears from some members of the group.

However, it was the next question that brought out the most powerful responses of the night: "What is something that you wish everyone knew about you, before they could ever judge your character?" our senior counselor Jon asked the group.

A flood of stories was unleashed; stories of abuse, bitter divorce, suicide and depression caused even our strongest members to succumb to tears. I did my best to stop the torrent of tears flowing down my own face when it was my turn to speak. With little knowledge of what I was going to say, I began.

"What I wish people could know about me is that… I have three gay uncles. They have had so many challenges to overcome because of their sexual orientation. The last thing they need is for people to disrespect their lifestyle in their everyday language. I can't stand it when people call something "gay" when they don't like it. I wish people knew that their word choice hurts me, and it hurts my family." I choked out the last line through my renewed tears. Several people put their arms around me and patted my back.

I felt my previously shaking hands steady themselves as I realized what I had finally been able to share. I had never stood up against the use of offensive words before, even though they bothered me immensely. I had always assumed, as I still did for the next several days, that speaking out would make no difference; people would continue to use these words no matter what I had to say about it. However, this idea changed when I checked my mailbox two days later and found a note from a girl in my group who I had not spoken to very much.

> I had never stood up against the use of offensive words before, even though they bothered me immensely.

"I want to thank you. You've changed my life and made me realize I have been offending people with my words. You've made it clear to me that I need to change and I'm going to."

I sat in stunned silence as tears once again filled my eyes. For the first time in my sixteen years I felt like I had effected change. I was able to stop one person from offending people with her words, and from that experience I gained the belief that I can stop more than just one person. I am no longer scared to stand up for what I believe in. I know now that all it takes is one story and one person willing to listen to make change happen.

— Heidi Patton —
Chicken Soup for the Soul: Just for Teenagers

Speaking Up

A time comes when silence is betrayal.
~Dr. Martin Luther King, Jr.

I never looked up when my friends were talking and joking about the "Retarded Boy" (as they referred to him) a few tables away. It didn't even cross my mind that he might feel bad when people whispered about him, or that he might be hurt when he saw the weird, disgusted looks from his peers. So I just let them talk, and I never intervened.

Then came the day I was standing in the kitchen helping with dinner, asking my mom about my brother's doctor's appointment. They were testing him for autism. My parents had told me there was a huge chance of it coming out positive, but I had never thought about him like that. My brother, Captain, four years old at the time, had always been my best friend. We would wrestle, play games and have the best of times together, even though we were far apart in age. My mom told me about the appointment, and when she got to the point about the test, she stopped. I turned around and she had tears in her eyes. I stared at her, wishing she would say something, when I realized what that silence meant. My eyes got blurry and my breathing got very ragged. "The test came out positive, sweetheart," she said with a calm voice. I broke down, crying and asking why it had happened to Captain.

My mom was trying to pull me together, saying that Captain couldn't see me like this and I had to be a big girl, when the front door opened, and Captain, our three-year-old sister Cali, and my father came in. I walked out of the kitchen. Captain was talking to our dad and then stopped, switching his attention to me. As he looked up at me with those huge blue eyes, I had to look away. I couldn't look at him. Everything had just changed. He was no longer that little baby brother who was just a normal little boy anymore. He was a little boy with a disease who didn't deserve anything that was going to come with it.

Over time, I was able to accept his disease a little more. We had to move a while later because Captain needed treatment and where we lived at the time didn't have the type he needed. So we moved to Maryland. Time passed and Captain and I both started at a new school. One day, I was standing in the bus line waiting when the "short bus" came and picked some kids up. The children in the other line started making jokes about the "retards" on that bus and I felt a strange feeling in my stomach. One that I had never felt before. As the other kids laughed about the cruel jokes, I said, quietly, that those comments weren't very nice. No one listened and I went on my way. I regretted it immediately, and wished I had said something else.

My family moved once more to a new school and I was

given my chance to speak up pretty quickly. During band class, my teacher, Mrs. Young, stopped our playing to give us some feedback.

"Guys, we're playing like the kids on the short bus! Come on!" I felt that same feeling I had on the bus line, except worse. This was an adult, and I thought adults would

> **Apparently, ignorance comes in all different ages.**

be more careful about what they said. Apparently, ignorance comes in all different ages. The entire room was laughing when I raised my hand. I wasn't sure what I was going to say but I wanted to be heard.

"Yes, Alexis?" Mrs. Young asked. The class quieted down because the new girl was about to talk for the first time. I could feel my face getting red and was about to just say never mind, when my mouth opened and this came out:

"I don't think we should make fun of the short bus, because there are a lot of people on that bus who have great personalities and have the same feelings we do." I could feel my voice getting louder. "And also, I know some people on those buses and they are some of the most caring, sweetest, and smartest people so I would appreciate it if you didn't make fun of them."

The room was very quiet and everyone stared at me. Mrs. Young apologized for the comment and then started the song again. Everyone was a little on edge. At the end of the class, everyone was giving me weird looks and sizing me up. They looked like they were labeling me a nerd right off the bat, but I didn't care, because I knew three things: I had spoken

> I had spoken the truth and what others in the class were probably thinking.

the truth and what others in the class were probably thinking, I had taught everyone something, and while everyone in the classroom was being a follower, I had decided to take a different path. I want to become a leader and a positive role model and go on to teach others about people on the "short bus." I want to teach people about my brother Captain, who doesn't know that he's different. And really, he's not. He's just a five-year-old who loves baseball and eating cookies, and I never want to hear anybody make fun of him.

— Alexis Streb —
Chicken Soup for the Soul: Just for Teenagers

Speak up
Stand up
Step up

Room 8

As we work to create light for others,
we naturally light our own way.
~Mary Anne Radmacher

When I was in seventh grade my study hall was extremely tedious and as much fun as getting shot with spitballs or having immense wads of papers hurled at your head. It was not for me.

I went to see my guidance counselor, Mrs. Greig. We discussed the various paths I could take to avoid study hall, from being a volunteer gym assistant to being an office helper.

I know that being a gym assistant sounds super exciting, but running three miles seems just as bad to me as feeling a spitball running down my neck. The option I chose to avoid study hall was helping out in an "artistic classroom."

The next day I wore a nasty old shirt to school so I wouldn't ruin a good one in art class. Along with that I wore stained pants with holes all over and shoes that had mud caked all over them. I looked as if I had been living on the street.

When seventh period rolled around Mrs. Greig took me to

Room 8, the artistic classroom. When we got to the door, this gorgeous lady stood there. She was a little taller than average height, had beautiful soft brown hair, and was wearing a black dress. She did not look like she was dressed to lead an art class.

She said, "Hi! My name is Mrs. Magee. Welcome to Room 8, the autistic support classroom."

I said, "Don't you mean the artistic classroom?"

She smiled and replied, "Well they can be colorful sometimes, but I'm pretty sure I'm teaching a self-contained autistic support classroom. I know nothing about art."

I felt like a gargantuan idiot. Who else would get those two words messed up but me? I stood silently with my arms behind my back staring at the freshly waxed floors.

Mrs. Magee welcomed me with a warm smile. Then she introduced me to the students, who all rushed to greet me. I walked in and became their friend. I stayed until the bell rang.

When I got home, I bawled. I had always heard so many disagreeable things about that classroom. The students did not look like my classmates. They did not talk like my classmates either. The students talked in brief sentences. How could I help them? I doubted my abilities and myself.

My parents told me to give it one more day.

I would have rather been a gym teacher's assistant than have that feeling. I thought about going back to study hall. My parents told me to give it one more day.

The next day I dragged my feet down the hallway as I reported for duty at Room 8. Mrs. Magee greeted me and then said, "If you have any questions about autism just ask."

That day I worked with a senior named Erika. She had long dark hair and a beautiful smile. I helped her with math, and that was the day something changed in me.

Maybe it was because she was like a child trapped inside an adult's body. Maybe it was because I saw that I was able to help her, or maybe it was because without knowing it, Erika captured my heart in an unexplainable way.

Whatever it was it changed my future.

I volunteered up until graduation day when I said goodbye in tears. These kids were my family. I took Roger's face in my hands. He was the most popular student in the class. He was crying too, but he smiled as he grabbed his backpack and walked out the door for summer vacation. "See you next year, Britt." I just waved goodbye; I couldn't explain to him that I would not be returning.

I glanced around the room and saw Chris, a game show fanatic, repeating questions from *Jeopardy!*. I smiled and tried to fight back the lump in my throat.

The last one in the room was Jarrett, the guy I took to the senior prom. I reminisced about the cheers we got walking down the aisle for the Grand March. We had linked arms as I whispered, "Left, right, left, step, step, step."

Quickly I snapped back to reality.

These were the faces I was afraid of when I started middle school.

My friends in Room 8 taught me more about myself than I would have ever learned without them. Room 8 brought me joy… and a career. I am going to be that teacher in the black dress. And I am going to tell the students who do not have disabilities about what makes the kids in Room 8 and all the other Room 8's out there special.

I cannot remember telephone numbers after hearing them once like Justin can.

I cannot get a crowd on its feet quicker than Roger can.

I cannot remember the exact questions and answers to a game show like Chris can.

I cannot take apart electronics and put them back together like Matt can.

> My friends in Room 8 taught me more about myself than I would have ever learned without them.

I cannot solve as hard a math problem as Nate can.

I cannot love horses like Erika can.

I cannot remember every part of a car and what it entails like Robbie can.

I can, however, tell their story.

Our story.

— Brittany Autumn Austin —
Chicken Soup for the Soul: Think Possible

Chapter 4

MAKE THE EFFORT

Math

God does not care about our mathematical
difficulties. He integrates empirically.
—Albert Einstein

When I was in seventh grade, my parents paid forty dollars a week for a tutor to come to my house and help me with math, which ended up raising my mark from a fifty to a... fifty-five.

Okay, maybe it was partly my fault. Maybe I should have spent less time worrying about that oh-so-important geography assignment and more time plotting my y-intercepts. But math is a tricky thing. And sitting down at a chair to work on confusing algebraic equations for two hours is a slow and painful process, usually involving unexplained fidgeting of the fingers and numerous trips to the refrigerator in an attempt to get off that chair for at least five minutes. Take it from me, you get used to teachers always leaning over your desk during tests, and visits from past teachers always prompted the million-dollar question: "How's math?"

So I became afraid of it. While normal people my age

> **I became afraid of anything to do with numbers.**

were scared of spiders and that new ride at Wonderland, I became afraid of anything to do with numbers. The thought of a teacher picking on me in class was terrifying. The red marking — which might as well have been a painting drawn by my math teacher for all the ink he used on that stupid test — was like a component in a horror movie, where I often felt like cutting that test up and then screaming my head off, another component in horror movies. It only got worse in ninth grade. Every report card I ever received was delivered with the comment: "Victoria needs to ask for assistance in class." But I couldn't tell my teachers the real reason why I didn't ask for help: I didn't want to be a dummy. Every question I had was, in my opinion at the time, something that the entire class got and I didn't understand. So instead, I resorted to the mindset of not caring about anything and concluding that everything would work out in the end.

It didn't.

After spending a semester not caring about homework and not trying on tests, still afraid of math and convinced I would never succeed, my math teacher called one summer morning to tell me I would spend the next three weeks at school,

> **As it turned out, I failed tenth grade math.**

redoing the entire course so I could pass. As it turned out, I failed tenth grade math. With flying colours, I might add.

This news was met with sudden tears, a loud "this can't

be happening to me!" and a refusal to do anything related to friends, family, fun, or life. I took to my books. English rules and math drools. I had morphed into some ridiculous failure, destined for a life of disappointment, because I would never graduate and never go to university and never, never, do anything good in my life.

That's when it hit me. Why was I scared of a bunch of numbers, anyway? Why was I so petrified of asking my teacher for help? Because I was afraid of looking like a moron? Why did I barely study for tests because I had convinced myself I would never do well? Who was this unconfident student and what happened to that determined, confident teenager I had once been?

I finally realized that I had let math take over my life. Sure, I still don't like numbers, and I probably never will. But if it's one thing I've learned, it's that math is just a subject. There was really no reason to be afraid of it — I just needed to take the bull by the horns. Face the music. Be the bigger person! Gradually, my attitude changed, and I became more positive once I let go of my mathematic fears.

> **There was really no reason to be afraid of it—I just needed to take the bull by the horns.**

So I'm off to three weeks of summer school, three hours of math each day. If there's any bright side, it's that at least I have some sort of self-esteem embedded in me, somewhere, and I'll be getting the help I need. After all, maybe next year I'll be doing better because I studied more often in the summer than the other kids at school. Maybe failing wasn't the worst thing that could have happened.

So gone are my days of imagining numbers as something to be afraid of and thinking that algebra is out to get me. Substitution, elimination, factoring—here I come.

—Victoria Linhares—
Chicken Soup for the Soul: Just for Teenagers

The Christmas Witch

Peace on earth will come to stay,
when we live Christmas every day.
–Helen Steiner Rice

*E*very kid in my neighborhood knew about the Christmas Witch. She was an elderly woman who left her Christmas decorations up all year long: a twinkling tree in the living room, a plastic wreath on the front door, and giant candy canes hanging in the windows. One kid told me the decorations were meant to coax youngsters closer to the house so the Christmas Witch could kidnap them.

I promised myself I would never go near that place, but when I turned fourteen, I got a newspaper route and discovered I'd have to deliver papers to the Christmas Witch.

"Stop worrying," my mother advised. "Just deliver the newspaper. She won't bother you."

My first day of delivery was a dark, frosty March morning.

The sky was just turning pink as I approached the last house on my route… that of the Christmas Witch.

Inside, the house was dark, so I tiptoed up the porch steps and placed the newspaper by the door.

I'd done it.

Then I quickly turned around, not seeing an icy spot on the step. I slipped, fell and slid down the stairs, landing on the sidewalk. I got up and stumbled, unable to walk. I'd sprained my ankle.

The porch light blinked on. The door opened. Someone shuffled out.

It was the Christmas Witch.

"I'm sorry," I said. "I…"

"Dear me," said the Christmas Witch. "Are you alright?"

Speechless, I pointed at my ankle.

"Come in; make sure you're okay." She smiled — not a wicked-witch smile but a nice smile, like she was concerned.

I didn't have any choice; I couldn't walk home. Holding the railing, I hobbled up the steps into her house. She turned on a living room lamp as I limped to a chair.

"Relax. I'll get something to warm you up." She hurried into the kitchen and returned a moment later, handing me a steaming mug. "Have some tea while I call your parents."

I told her my number as she dialed.

"Hello," she said. "This is Mona Wright on Pine Way Avenue. Your son slipped and hurt his ankle." She nodded and hung up. "Your mother will be here shortly."

"Thank you, Mrs. Wright."

"You're welcome." She sat down across from me, and then whispered, "You don't have to call me Mrs. Wright; you can call me Christmas Witch."

I was flabbergasted.

"It's alright." She shrugged. "I hear what people say. It doesn't matter."

"You do have lots of decorations," I said.

"I think it's pretty," she replied.

I said, "People think it's… weird."

"They don't understand the reason I leave up my decorations," she responded.

Like most teenagers, I just blurted out the next question. "What is the reason?"

Mrs. Wright took a deep breath. "Well, in 1970, my son Anthony was drafted and sent to Vietnam. He kept in touch with me as often as he could. My husband had died years earlier when Anthony was little, so the only family we had was each other. Anthony was scheduled to come home on leave on January 10, 1972. He called me on New Year's Eve and told me to leave up the Christmas decorations. He would help me put them away when he got home."

> "They don't understand the reason I leave up my decorations."

"So what happened?" I asked.

"Three days later, Anthony was killed in a helicopter crash," said Mrs. Wright. "My boy never made it back home. And even though I know it doesn't change anything, I can't bring myself to take down those decorations, even after all these years. I guess I just like to pretend that Anthony will be home soon

> **She was a sad, isolated person struggling with a terrible loss.**

to help me with that chore."

I didn't like myself at that moment. Mrs. Wright wasn't a witch. She was a sad, isolated person struggling with a terrible loss.

"I'm sorry," I said quietly.

Mrs. Wright sighed. "It felt good to talk about Anthony again."

The doorbell chimed.

"That's your mother," said Mrs. Wright, wiping her eyes.

My sprained ankle healed quickly, and my first morning back to delivering newspapers, Mrs. Wright met me at her door.

She smiled as I handed her the paper and said how much she enjoyed our visit.

Over the next couple of years, I saw Mrs. Wright occasionally, and I would always wave hello or stop to chat. Funny, I didn't think of her as the Christmas Witch anymore.

When I came home from my first semester of college, I learned that Mrs. Wright had passed away. I didn't get to see her again, but I never forgot her story.

After all these years, that experience has always helped me remember that ageless lesson: be a little less judgmental and a bit more understanding toward others.

— David Hull —
Chicken Soup for the Soul: The Wonder of Christmas

A Greyhound Encounter

*In helping others, we shall help ourselves,
for whatever good we give out completes
the circle and comes back to us.*
~Flora Edwards

When I tell people I'm shy, they tend not to believe me. I don't come across as a quiet, introverted person, but there is more to shyness than that. I do love to meet new people, make new friends and help a stranger here or there, but I am usually hindered by my anxiety, which prevents me from going over and making an effort.

That was why a seemingly innocuous encounter on the Greyhound bus meant so much to me. It showed me that I could indeed get past myself and reach out.

It was an overnight trip from Ohio to New York, and I was taking it with a few friends of mine from the boarding school I was attending. I was headed home to surprise my family for the holidays and was pretty excited about it.

We settled into our seats for the long ride ahead, well-stocked with candy and an optimistic pillow or two. The passengers formed quite the motley assortment, a microcosm of our great, diverse nation. The bus slowly settled down for the night, as each of us tried to make ourselves as comfortable as possible. A majority of us tried finding comfortable sleeping positions as a peaceful silence descended upon the lumbering bus.

And then, the silence was pierced by a decidedly unhappy wail. It was an infant, and he was crying. Loudly. His father attempted desperately to shush him, but to no avail. He seemed unsure of what to do, how to handle this precious bundle in his arms. And he was all alone.

I wondered what would cause a man so young to be traveling alone with an infant. My heart went out to him; he looked ready to cry himself. And that baby just broke my heart.

So I turned to my friends, and with a conviction so unlike me, I said, "I am going to that baby!"

> **This was so beyond my comfort zone that I couldn't even see my comfort zone with binoculars.**

They looked at me like I was crazy and then proceeded to tell me that I was. I believed them, truthfully. This was so beyond my comfort zone that I couldn't even see my comfort zone with binoculars.

But there was a baby. And he was crying. And that was all that mattered.

So I took a step out of my comfortable seat and a running leap outside my comfort zone and I approached that hapless dad.

"Here, let me try," I said.

His look echoed my friends', but his had the extra element of sheer desperation. He looked around the bus, almost as if to ensure that it was okay to entrust his baby to a stranger, and saw that there was nowhere for me to go anyway. He shrugged and wordlessly handed the baby to me.

> We made quite the sight—me, an Orthodox young woman singing the age-old Jewish bedtime song to an African-American infant.

I took the distraught boy back to my seat and slowly began rocking him in my arms. I sang the lullaby I had grown up with in his ears.

We made quite the sight — me, an Orthodox young woman singing the age-old Jewish bedtime song to an African-American infant. People looked up, gaped, and then either smiled at the prospect of peace and quiet, or shrugged nonchalantly at just another night on Greyhound.

After a few moments, the baby relaxed in my arms and let his eyelids flutter to the rhythm of my lullaby. And then, miraculously, he was asleep.

I handed him back to the relieved father, who placed him carefully in his infant seat.

"Thank you," he whispered.

"No, thank *you*," I responded.

—Devora Adams—

Chicken Soup for the Soul: Step Outside Your Comfort Zone

The Pin

*I love to see a young girl go out and grab
the world by the lapels.*
—Maya Angelou

Ever since joining my high school's wrestling team, I
dreamed of pinning a boy. I knew that it was rather
farfetched as I was smaller and weaker than the
boys in my weight class, who appeared to have been
training for wrestling ever since they were born. After being
unable to compete freshman year due to a serious concussion, I made it my mission to pin a boy during my sophomore year, and every second I spent at practice was another
second I was closer to achieving my dream.

That victory would come sooner than I expected.

In early January, my team was invited to participate in a
tournament at a local high school. Despite losing all my matches
so far in the season, I remember feeling rather optimistic that
my dream would come true as I packed my singlet and headgear
into my duffel bag.

My first match in the tournament was over in two minutes.

I was near the edge of the ring, sprawling with my legs stretched out far from my body. But in an instant the boy had hooked his arm around my leg and toppled me over to my back, pinning me. I lost my second match too.

By this point in the tournament, I was exhausted, both physically and emotionally. I wanted to give up and go home. But then I gave myself a lecture: "You don't practice two hours each day to go home," I thought, preparing for my third match. "You practice to succeed."

> **I wanted to give up and go home.**

As I stepped onto the mat with my opponent, I took a moment to observe him. He was around my height and definitely stronger. Nervously, I shook his hand, starting the match.

We spent the first few seconds tugging and pulling on each other, snapping each other's heads down. Thinking I had the opportunity to shoot, I took a shot — lurching forward as I glided my knees across the mat and grasped his leg. Within an instant, he sprawled, kicking his legs back and dropping his weight on me. I struggled to hold onto his leg, feeling my fingers slipping as he continued to stretch his legs back and dig his hips into my neck. So instead of holding on, I decided to slide out from under him.

Quickly, I moved my right leg and slid out from under him. He fell on to the mat, and as he sprang back up, I heard cheers around the mat as the spectators realized that it was a girl who had slid out of a boy's grasp.

I felt my confidence growing. The second round had started.

I started on my knees and had to scramble onto my feet. He made an attempt to lock me in his arms, and I successfully peeled myself away from him. We continued to pull and tug at each other's arms as we contemplated what to do next.

By the third round I was out of breath, and I began to fear I'd lose out of pure exhaustion. But as he made a grab for me, I managed to slip around him and wrap my arms around his torso, making a quick but sturdy butterfly grip.

I tried lifting him off the ground by bumping his hip with mine. He just teetered forward, too big for me to lift him. Instead, I turned my body in a corkscrew-like motion, twisting him to the ground as I landed on top of him. My heart hammered in my chest. I kept my knees off the ground as I continued to apply pressure by digging my hips into his broad back. I felt him flatten under me, and I continued to push harder as I gasped for air, completely aware of all the eyes staring at me.

As my coaches and teammates shouted words of encouragement, I shuffled around him to line up with his side. Quickly, he lifted up his arm so that his elbow made a bend as he started to get off the mat. Yet all those hours of practice flooded back to me in a split second and I fiercely hooked my arm into his and began to drive forward so that he, once lying on his stomach, was beginning to turn over onto his back.

"Stay off your knees!" I heard someone shout.

"Keep pushing!" another person roared.

The referee got down on the mat as I felt my opponent's

shoulder touch the mat. I locked my feet in place, my legs shaking as I struggled to apply pressure by staying off my knees. I could feel him squirm under me, and the referee began the countdown to a pin.

The referee slapped the mat once.

I made my grasp around the boy tighter.

He slapped the mat again.

I looked up at the ceiling — "counting the ceiling tiles" as my coaches put it, so my chest would apply pressure to my opponent.

He slapped the mat again.

I could feel sweat dripping from my hair cap, my body almost crumbling from exhaustion.

The whole gymnasium erupted in cheers.

The referee blew the whistle with a final slap, and the whole gymnasium erupted in cheers.

"I did it," I thought, pulling myself off my opponent. I was practically beaming as I realized what I had just done. "I pinned a boy!"

The referee grabbed my arm and lifted it in the air, signifying my victory.

I was a champion, and everyone on the bleachers could see it. And even though I didn't place in that tournament, I accomplished my personal goal. All the hours of sweat and exhaustion I had endured through practice had led up to that sweet moment of success. But my greatest victory that day was not my win, but my realization that by working hard, I could do anything I set my mind to, no matter how impossible it might seem.

— Madison Kurth —
Chicken Soup for the Soul: Think Possible

A Dance with Destiny

Dancing is like dreaming with your feet!
~Constanze

My mother was a drug addict. She was deemed unfit to care for me, so my single grandmother raised me from birth. My father was incarcerated during most of my childhood, like a lot of kids I knew. I grew up in the projects in East Harlem, New York. Drugs, gangs, violence, it was a dangerous place to be a kid, especially a small kid. But I was strong, I was fast, and I was motivated — so pretty early on I learned to be as big and bad as I had to be. My life depended on it. We were church-going people, but I have to admit that antisocial behavior, belligerence, and fighting occupied much of my early years.

Church was the one peaceful place I knew. I always loved the music. My cousin Journee was in the praise dance group, and when watching her dance I felt something beautiful bloom inside me.

But back outside on the street, in the "'hood," it was same ol', same ol'. I spent time mouthing off and fighting other boys to gain respect. Of course I was a difficult student — although I was intelligent, teachers had a hard time with me. I made sure of that. The school principal got tired of telling me to shape up. I had no purpose and I was going nowhere. I pretended I didn't care.

> **I had no purpose and I was going nowhere.**

A school field trip to see the Dance Theatre of Harlem saved my life. Those dancers on the stage seemed superhuman. Their every movement thrilled me to the core. I wanted to do that. I wanted to be that. My first experience with classical ballet moved me to make a deal with my principal: if I promised to stop fighting, behave myself, and pull my grades up, she would contact the dance company and arrange an audition for me. Within a year, I had a full scholarship to the Dance Theatre of Harlem School. Dance became my safe place, my secret place, a place where I didn't feel the need to prove how big and bad I was.

I was focused and disciplined, and the teachers at DTH noticed. I progressed quickly. I had a talent for remembering choreography and could jump very high. From my years on the streets I had developed strength and agility beyond that of most of the other young dancers. After additional training at Ballet Academy East, Boston Ballet and Jacob's Pillow, after graduating with good grades from high school at age seventeen, I signed my first professional contract — with the Dance Theatre of Harlem ensemble. My dream had become reality. I began performing immediately on the DTH 40th Anniversary Tour.

The tour mission was to bring dance to communities that might have never seen ballet before. We were bringing a message of hope and inspiration to damaged youth in those communities, and I felt a personal responsibility to be on that stage. I wanted to inspire someone — one kid — the way I had been inspired. I felt I was representing something much larger than myself. I had a purpose.

> **At age seventeen, I signed my first professional contract—with the Dance Theatre of Harlem ensemble.**

I received a mandate from my hero, the legendary Arthur Mitchell, at Dance Theatre of Harlem. According to him, it's my mission and destiny to live "in service to the art form" — and, to me, that means a lifetime commitment to giving back, in any way I can.

Now I am in my third season with the Los Angeles Ballet. It has been my privilege to perform solo parts in both *The Nutcracker* and *Swan Lake* throughout Los Angeles County. And it's also my privilege to work with disadvantaged youth in low-income neighborhoods around Southern California as a part of Los Angeles Ballet's Power of Performance! (POP!) program, which brings hundreds of underprivileged children to performances, free of charge, through a network of community service organizations.

Sometimes when I injure my knee or sprain an ankle — it

comes with the job — I feel like I want to cancel a performance. But I think of those kids from the "'hood" who are coming to the show, and I have to be on that stage. I want them to see their own reflection, to see themselves up there. The house lights go down, the curtain rises, and as I dance I know that there is someone out there in the dark, from one of those neighborhoods, needing a little inspiration. I'll be there to give it to them.

— Christopher Charles McDaniel —
Chicken Soup for the Soul: From Lemons to Lemonade

Chapter 5

FACE YOUR CHALLENGES

The Mirror Girl

Anorexia is an awful thing, but you get
yourself into it, and only you can get
yourself out of it.
~Celia Imrie

"Ugh. Look at that flab hanging from your arms, and the padded ring circling your hips. Disgusting! And your thighs? You call those muscular? I call it 'you look like you could use forty minutes on the treadmill and a cup of green juice.'"

I muttered insults to the fifteen-year-old girl staring back at me from the mirror. Most of us would never say these comments to another human being, but this mirror girl was hideous. I grabbed a sweatshirt to conceal the uncomely body, inside of which I was stuck.

I reached high school, and self-doubt smacked me every chance that it could. Walking down the dull, blue halls was a nightmare. The pretty girls were getting prettier, the popular girls were radiating with confidence, and the smart girls were just smart. They stood in their groups, confidence pouring from their smiles, laughs, and funny jokes. And there I was, blending in with the lockers. I was a nobody — an unnoticed girl whose body seemed to have undergone an overnight change that left me feeling like a cow. I told myself, *You're not cool enough to hang out with those people. They don't want to talk to you, why would they? You're nothing special.*

The negative self-talk was crushing me. Until I realized that maybe there was a way I could turn this

> ## The negative self-talk was crushing me.

around. Maybe there was a way that I too, could be beautiful, confident, and popular. I hunted for an answer. What did the pretty girls have that I didn't have? Slimness. What did the popular girls have that I didn't have? Slenderness! Skinny was the common thread, the answer to my self-doubt.

At that moment, I put thinness on a pedestal. I idolized every girl, every model, every actress who was smaller than me, and I envied her slim build. My dad always said that our family was big-boned. At that moment, I despised my big bones. So I set out on a quest to satisfy the hunger that I most craved: a thin body. Then I could be happy, confident and beautiful.

"Starting today, no more sweets, chips or soda. And you have to exercise, every day."

The mirror girl looked disappointed, but I was satisfied with my decision to transform her into something worth looking at. I refused to eat junk, and I kept a daily log of my calories. I wrote down everything I ate. It gave me peace of mind to know how many calories I had consumed. It determined whether

I could eat a meal, or if I had to skip it. Soon, I saw results, and so did others.

"Mal, you lost weight! You look good," they said.

I was ecstatic. People noticed. I couldn't lose my momentum. I had to maintain my strict diet and exercise routine. But soon, things took a downward turn.

It was a Friday night, in February. I could hear the phone ringing. I was hoping in my head that it wasn't for me. My mom picked it up. It was for me. "Hello?" I mustered up what enthusiasm I could. "Hey Mal! It's Hayley. Me, Sophie and Riley are going out to grab a pizza tonight. Would you like to come?" Why were my friends inviting me to partake in food-related activities? I didn't eat pizza anymore.

"I'm sorry Hayley, I told my sister I'd hang out with her tonight. I can't." It was an excuse. Truthfully, I didn't want to tell her that consuming a slice of greasy, cheesy, fattening pizza would be like digging myself into a hole of guilt and regret.

> **Food had become my enemy.**

Food had become my enemy.

"That's okay! Maybe next time. Talk to you later."

"Talk to you later." I hung up the phone and went downstairs to my bedroom. I closed the door, and turned to face the mirror girl.

"You could afford to lose some of that belly fat. Your thighs are still huge. If you don't keep working out, those flabby arms are coming back for you!"

The mirror hung on the back of my bedroom door, and

there I stayed, locked away from the temptation of food, so that I could reach my ideal of thinness.

One afternoon, my mother took me to a clinic where I met with a doctor, then a dietician. At 92 pounds, I was about 30 pounds underweight. At some point, I was diagnosed with anorexia nervosa. I had never felt more accomplished. My clothes were loose-fitting, my arms were sticks, my stomach was concave, my cheekbones were jagged. I didn't care about the self-starvation; I had molded myself into society's definition of beauty. I looked like the models and the skinny girls; I was there.

But what had I truly accomplished? Was I confident? Beautiful? Happy?

One afternoon, I walked down to my bedroom and caught a glance of the mirror girl. The girl I saw, the reflection, was someone I didn't recognize. She looked hollow, exhausted, and angry. She looked lifeless. Her image made me stop. Was this my idea of perfection? Was this beauty, confidence and happiness? At that moment, I saw the price that I was paying for thinness, and I realized that price was much too high.

I was slipping away as a student, a friend, a sibling, and a daughter. I no longer figure skated — I had given up my passion. I stopped living life because I was too cold, too exhausted, too afraid that I'd miss a workout. I feared food and felt compelled to check the scale every hour to make sure I hadn't gained a pound. I was living a life of obsessive, fearful misery. And worse than harming myself, I was hurting those who cared.

Luckily, my friends and family never stopped supporting

me. I am forever grateful for them because otherwise, I don't think I ever would have snapped out of this detrimental cycle. In time, they helped me put body image and food back into perspective. I began figure skating again, and I learned that food would not make me fat, but that it would give me the energy I needed to fulfill my passions and to live life.

> **In cherishing our own flaws, imperfections and uniqueness lies our true beauty.**

Since that period of time, I've never looked at the mirror girl in the same way. I've never insulted her, or hurt her. I decided that from then on, I had to treat this mirror girl with respect. I celebrated her beauty, despite her imperfections; and from this experience I learned one of the most critical lessons about beauty, confidence and happiness. It is that in cherishing our own flaws, imperfections and uniqueness lies our true beauty, and once we embrace ourselves for who we are rather than what we look like, without regard for what others think, do we truly become our most confident and happiest selves.

— Mallory Lavoie —
Chicken Soup for the Soul: Curvy & Confident

FUEL GOOD
FEEL GOOD

USA vs. My Mom

The turning point in the process of
growing up is when you discover
the core of strength within you that
survives all hurt.
~Max Lerner

In 2012, 1,276,099 people were arrested for possession of a controlled substance in the United States, according to one website that I researched. My mother was one of them. I would have never thought my mom would end up in prison over prescription medication. I didn't know you could get addicted to something a doctor prescribed. But ever since my parents separated in 2007, my mom had abused her prescription medication.

Mom has been diagnosed with a number of things, including scoliosis and depression. Along with those diagnoses came several medicines: Oxycontin, Percocet, and Xanax are a few that come to mind. These are highly addictive medications. I believe her addiction started when I was in sixth grade. Her friends would come over, and she'd tell me to go to my room because they were having "adult talk." I wasn't ignorant as to what was really going on; I knew she abused her medicine. She crushed up her pills and used a straw or a broken pen to snort them. Once I asked why she didn't just take them by mouth and she replied that they worked faster when she snorted them. I didn't really understand why she needed the medicine.

Mom had a new boyfriend when I was in seventh grade. He paid for our apartment, bought her a car, and always made sure we had food and necessities. He seemed like an okay guy, but then I found out that he abused prescription medication too. They were both looking for a better life and somehow they thought that abusing drugs was the answer. They were always nodding off. Holding a conversation with them was nearly impossible. They would drool and mumble things to themselves. Their eyes would roll back and their bodies were lifeless at all hours of the day. If they even started to come down from their high, they would do more drugs.

> **My mom wasn't my mom anymore.**

My mom wasn't my mom anymore. I became angry; I was tired of watching her do that to herself. It was as if she had just forgotten about me, like she didn't care about me anymore. I would come home from school and find her passed out. I would run to her with tears rolling down my face because I thought she was dead.

Then my mom and her boyfriend started to sell prescription medications. A guy would give them a certain amount to sell, and they would bring the money back to him and get a piece of it. They claimed it was just "easy money" until they got back on their feet and got real jobs. We always had random people coming and going at our house. This happened throughout the day and even during the night.

Sometime after they started dealing, my mom and her boyfriend began making trips with groups of people to Florida. In Florida, they would all visit multiple doctors' offices as new patients, get prescriptions, and then go to multiple pharmacies to get the scripts filled. My mom made these trips several times a year. She was trafficking drugs across state lines, a federal offense. In 2011, a group of six people, including my mom, split up into two vehicles and drove down to Florida. On their return, the Georgia State Police pulled over one of the vehicles — the one that my mom wasn't in.

I don't know exactly what happened, but they were released and drove back to Kentucky. About a month later, they were arrested in Somerset, Kentucky and held in Pulaski County Detention Center. The police offered them a deal — if they named the others involved in the drug activity, they would get reduced sentences. So, they spoke out against my mom and the others involved. On January 31, 2012, a U.S. Marshall found my mother and arrested her. I found out via text message that my mother had been taken to jail. It was the worst day of my life.

I would go to Pulaski County Detention Center about twice a week to see my mom. You were only allowed thirty-minute visits, and you had to sit behind a glass window and talk through a nasty telephone that didn't work half the time. Most of our visits ended in tears or fights.

My mom went before the judge on September 11, 2012 and pleaded guilty to the drug charges. I went with my grandmother to watch the trial. We sat in the last row and saw my mom enter through the side door in handcuffs and foot cuffs, as if she were a dangerous criminal. She started crying when she saw me, and I did too. I will never forget when the judge asked her if she had anything else to say. Despite the judge's warning not to look into the seats behind her, my mom turned to face me. With tears rolling down her cheeks, she apologized and told me how much she loved me. It absolutely broke my heart.

The judge sentenced her to fifty-seven to seventy-one months in prison, due to the counts and her criminal history. At first it didn't hit me that it would be a long time until my mom was back in my life. But now, two years into her sentence, I realize how much time together we have lost; time that we will never get back.

My mom used to be a powerful, independent, lovely woman. She was a single mom, had a job and a house. She was even thinking about going to college to further her education in childcare. Now, she is residing in a federal prison camp, about eight hours away from me. We usually get five-minute phone calls once a week. I haven't seen my mom in over a year. I haven't hugged my mom since January 1, 2012.

I can't help but wonder what our lives could have been like if she hadn't

> I can't help but wonder what our lives could have been like if she hadn't used prescription drugs.

used prescription drugs. I watched her ruin her life with prescription medication, and because of that, I will never have a normal life. My mom hasn't had a chance to see me go to my high school proms. She hasn't been there to help me through the most important times in a teenage girl's life. I graduated high school in May of 2014, and my mom wasn't able to see it. I started college in August of 2014, and she missed that too.

It has had a huge impact on me, but I have come out on top of this situation. I took AP classes in high school, while also holding down a part-time job and participating in extracurricular school activities. My family has told me that they don't know how I'm living with this, that they would break if they were put in my position. But in all reality, you can't stop living when you have a life-changing experience. Life goes on, and someday it's going to get better. I don't feel sorry for myself. I accomplish a lot more that way.

— McKenzie Vaught —
Chicken Soup for the Soul: Find Your Inner Strength

Sunshine State

*How beautiful a day can be
when kindness touches it!*
~George Elliston

Growing up knowing that I was different was not easy. The realization that you're gay creeps up on you and then one day you recognize the lie that you've been living. My sudden realization came in high school.

I went to school in Florida with kids who made their distaste for gay people known and it scared me every day. I quickly understood what being gay meant. It meant living a lie. I had to restrain myself from being me, making sure to not be too flamboyant, or talk in an effeminate way, or comment on someone's cute shoes, or hold my partner's hand in public.

In many ways this is what led to my depression. My parents tried talking to me, but as a teen, talking to my parents didn't feel like an option. Looking back now, I wish I would have said something. They asked if I wanted to see a psychologist and I told them no. Nobody really wants to talk about the problems they have.

> **I struggled every day, trying to suppress my true self.**

I struggled every day, trying to suppress my true self, and as a result I became more depressed. Being a naturally happy person, I hid away the "depressed me" when I was around people, but that façade cracks so easily. I would make fun of myself to make others happy, make them laugh, keep them entertained, while beneath the surface I thought about my own death.

Making others laugh made me seem like a happier person. But during this constant battle to appear normal, I found myself losing ground. I couldn't pretend anymore and I found myself arguing constantly with my friends, pushing them away by accident, which only made my depression worse.

In the tenth grade life got harder. I saw other kids come out to their families and get kicked out. I loved my family and never wanted to lose them because I was gay. So I didn't tell them who I really was.

I thought about suicide but it never became a real possibility until my best friend dropped me. She had decided that being friends with me, a gay boy, would hurt her chances of getting a boyfriend. For days I cried. I dreaded going to school alone, with absolutely no friends. I felt as though I had lost everything important to me because I was gay.

One evening, after a particularly rough day at school, I found myself shopping with my mom. I remember walking through the noisy crowd of teenagers, feeling them glare at me like I was a freak. I heard them whisper to each other, talking about what I wore, how I talked. It was like a nightmare come true. My mother was very perceptive and knew I was having a bad day and quickly tried to take my mind off it by shopping.

> I loved my family and never wanted to lose them because I was gay.

I dragged myself through the store right behind her, leaning on the cart, looking defeated. I couldn't do it anymore. I was planning my suicide for later that week.

As my mother searched the aisle for dinner, an elderly woman shuffled up beside me pushing her cart. She was short, had close-cut white hair, and her skin was wrinkled and freckled from too much time in the sun. Her eyes were steely gray. She reached her hand out to touch my cheek.

"It gets better, child," she whispered as she lay her wispy fingers on my disheartened face.

She gave me an empathetic grin and shuffled away, pushing her buggy full of toilet paper and milk. I swallowed hard and turned to my mother. I sputtered, asking if we could leave as tears began to run down my face. When we got into the car I lay down in the back, sobbing into the rough fabric of the seat.

I never really believed in fate, but some things are too surreal to be coincidence. That woman saved my life, and ever since then, her message has stuck with me. No one asked her to reach out to a stranger and tell him it gets better. No one asked her to save a life. All she did was say four words. She never knew me, she didn't know my name, or the weight I

> **That woman saved my life, and ever since then, her message has stuck with me.**

carried, and she will never know how big an impact those four words made. I wish I knew who she was so I could tell her how much she has changed me for the better.

I began to volunteer with hospice after that, hoping I would see her somewhere, just for the opportunity to thank her for being alive. But that is the thing about fate; it takes you by surprise and in its wake leaves lasting impressions. Sometimes you don't even know its name.

— Mike Ford —
Chicken Soup for the Soul: Random Acts of Kindness

What Doesn't Kill You Makes You Stronger

We shall draw from the heart of suffering
itself the means of inspiration and survival.
~Winston Churchill

I glanced at my best friend, Morgan, as she gave me a reassuring smile and said, "Don't worry honey. Everything's gonna be just fine." I smiled back weakly and once again began to stare down the door and check the time every ten seconds. Finally, the doctor came in.

"Let's take you back for some X-rays," he said.

I slowly followed him through the door and to a dark room where I was laid on a table.

"Okay. On three I need you to hold your breath for just a few seconds. You won't feel anything, so don't worry. Ready? One… Two… Three."

A few minutes later I was back in the examination room with Morgan and my dad. They both took turns telling me everything was going to be fine. I tried to believe them, but inside I had a feeling they were wrong. After what seemed like forever, the doctor returned and said three words that changed my life forever:

"She has scoliosis."

He lit up my X-ray film, which revealed my spine, which was in the shape of an S.

"Now the bottom curve is at thirty-five degrees, which is pretty significant, but they do not perform surgery unless it's over forty-five. I'm going to send you to a doctor in Denver, one of the best in the state."

When I heard I would not need surgery, I was relieved. Unfortunately, this relief didn't last long. My mom and dad took me to see the doctor in Denver a few weeks later. He took one look at me and shook his head in disappointment.

"That's not thirty-five degrees… that's probably closer to sixty… these are the wrong X-rays. We need to get one of you standing up."

So now I was in the same predicament. More X-rays. More waiting. More nervous feelings. When he came back with my new X-ray, I immediately felt my stomach drop.

"So… the bottom curve is actually fifty-seven degrees. And this top one is forty-three. And there's also this small one by your neck that's about ten degrees. Your only option is surgery."

After this, he said a lot more that I either didn't catch or just didn't understand. I was too upset. I was only fifteen years old, and I was going to have to go through one of the most intense surgeries possible. I couldn't hold it in any longer. I felt my eyes well with tears as they began streaming down my face. My mom hugged me close and whispered, "It's okay. We'll get you through this," as I cried into her shoulder.

Even more bad news. My insurance wouldn't cover anything if we continued to see this doctor. I had to switch to a new one in Colorado Springs.

> I was only fifteen years old, and I was going to have to go through one of the most intense surgeries possible.

That night, I looked at myself in the mirror with disgust. For the first time I noticed my uneven shoulders. My crooked back. There was no way I could get through this.

After a short visit to my new doctor in April, my surgery was set for July 26. Until then, I went to physical therapy once a week, and continued to participate in marching band at my school. Since I knew I would not be playing my flute on the marching field, I picked up playing the bells in the pit.

Surgery day came even faster than I expected. We got to the hospital and I was put into a gown. I was terrified. After a few hours, I was wheeled into the operating room. The number of people and the amount of commotion going on in that room was what scared me the most. It seemed surreal to me. A mask was placed over my nose and mouth with a very sweet smelling gas. Before I knew it, everything went black.

I woke up eight hours later with two titanium rods,

twenty-four screws, and a straight spine, with my parents hovering overhead. I had no idea where I was or what was going on. I didn't feel any pain, which I later found out was because of a nerve block. The two major curves in my spine went from fifty-seven and forty-three, to twenty and fifteen.

"Miranda? We're going to move you from recovery into your ICU room. Okay?"

I weakly nodded. My mouth felt so dry, I could not speak. That one nod of my head must have taken everything out of me, because I fell asleep again before I even got to my room.

I woke up again. Now I could talk.

"Mom? I'm thirsty," I said, as I once again noticed my dry mouth.

I was fed ice chips. Then a nurse came in and put a small device in my hand.

"If you begin to feel any pain, push this button for morphine. You can use it every fifteen minutes."

I nodded, right before falling asleep again.

I didn't wake up again until morning. After sleeping all night and not getting any pain medicine, I could now feel everything.

"This is it," I thought to myself. "I'm going to die here in this hospital."

I was given two units of blood. During the day I kept telling my parents, "I can't do this anymore... I just wish I was dead."

Later on the physical therapists came in to help me walk for the first time. I was not cooperative at all. I kept telling myself I couldn't do it. I needed help just to roll onto my side.

But do you know what I did? It took time, but I got up. And I walked. Even though it was with the help of others, the feeling was indescribable. Those few steps around the nurses' station changed my mood from "I can't," to "I will."

> **Those few steps around the nurses' station changed my mood from "I can't," to "I will."**

After that day, I recovered at a surprising rate. I was expected to be in the hospital for at least a week or two. I was released after four days. I was supposed to be bedridden for at least six months. I went back to marching band practice in two weeks, and back at school part-time in less than a month. Every time I accomplished something, it raised my confidence. Once I stopped looking at the glass as half empty, and saw everything in a more positive perspective, I got better faster than anyone had ever expected. Recovery for scoliosis surgery is typically about a year, but in a few months, I felt on top of the world.

Today, I continue to heal and recover. I am beginning physical therapy to get some of my old abilities back. I participate in marching band and yoga. I will admit things are not always easy. My spine can no longer bend or twist. But I find my way around things. With a positive outlook on what I have, I now know that there is nothing I cannot do. What doesn't kill you truly does make you stronger.

— Miranda Johnson, age 17 —
Chicken Soup for the Soul: The Power of Positive

Finding My Voice

**Panic at the thought of doing a
thing is a challenge to do it.
~Henry S. Haskins**

The bell rang. Students quieted as they settled into their seats. My English teacher stood in the front of the room, smiling and raising a book high.

"This week, we're reading Shakespeare's *Hamlet*," she said as her eyes sparkled.

Cool, I thought. I loved *A Midsummer Night's Dream* and *Romeo and Juliet*.

I should have held off on my excitement.

"The assignment will be for each of you to memorize the soliloquy, 'To Be or Not To Be,' and recite it to the class."

A few kids groaned. Some grinned. I looked down and watched my foot tap nervously as her words played over and over in my mind. Recite a soliloquy. To the class. That meant reading out loud, risking exposure. Panic gripped my heart and squeezed tight.

Some people struggle with stage fright, but I battled

something else. As long as I could remember, my enemy was my voice: "To B-B-Be or N-N-Not To B-B-B-Be," I imagined everyone staring while I painfully repeated sounds like a DJ scratching a record. Why did I have to stutter?

My stammer began when I was a preschooler. My mom and grandma encouraged me to speak slowly and thoughtfully. Sometimes, it worked. Sometimes, I spoke fluently without their prompting. Other times, I tripped over consonants and squinted as if the effort alone would will the words out.

In elementary school, my teacher, Mr. K, whisked me out of class a couple of times a week for speech therapy. We played vocal games. He taught me to elongate sounds, stutter freely, and keep going. He told me to maintain eye contact and believe in myself. Outside of family, few people even noticed I stuttered. My speech improved for a while.

Then, one day, the stuttering came back — more unpredictable and more distressing this time. I could be fluent one moment and struggle through talking with my mom the next. I thought

> **Then, one day, the stuttering came back.**

about the howls of laughter stuttering characters could elicit from movie and TV audiences. I didn't want to be a punch line. So I did what I had been taught to do when I wanted to know more about something: I read up on it.

My encyclopedia told me that three million people stuttered including James Earl Jones. Interesting. Wasn't he the voice of Darth Vader? Four times as many guys stuttered than girls. Great. Why did I have to break those odds?

I hadn't chosen to have a stutter. Even thinking my idea made me feel like a coward. But as I sat there, I came up with a solution to my stuttering problem. Hardly anyone knew that I stuttered. What if I kept it secret?

It wouldn't be that hard, I reasoned. Mostly, I was fluent. I could substitute synonyms for words I thought would trip me up. On bad days, I could clam up or pretend I didn't know the answers. It didn't take long for me to become a master at hiding my struggle with speech.

> The thought of being called on could make my heart pound and stomach drop.

But that choice came at a cost. The thought of being called on could make my heart pound and stomach drop. If I was asked to read, I nervously scanned the passage searching for words that might betray me. Then, there was a time when my trick wouldn't work. I was playing Mary in a church play and had a script to follow. I sat there thinking about the words and knew I would stutter on some of them. I couldn't change my lines. So I ran off the stage and cried.

Recite a soliloquy. To the class.

What if the same thing happened again? Or worse, what if nothing came out at all?

At home, I practiced in the mirror. I transformed myself into Hamlet for my mom and grandma. I took turns saying the speech with one of my friends. We laughed when we forgot words and cheered when we got through it.

But I never revealed my deepest worry. Alone in my room,

I pictured the worst. I saw my classmates' horrified looks as my eyes squinted, my hands balled into fists, and I stuttered over every word. I had never been teased because of my speech and that's how I wanted to keep it. I had enough drama coping with acne and figuring out boys. I didn't need people finishing my sentences and looking away when I talked.

Still, something nagged at me. I was tired of hiding, tired of feeling my stomach lurch and twist at the thought of speaking. There had to be another choice.

On the day when we were supposed to recite the monologues, I sat in English with my foot tapping, my mind focused on Hamlet's words. Some of my classmates nailed the speech. Others forgot parts or trembled through it.

When my turn came, I inhaled deeply and stood up. I had more on the line than they knew. I thought about the words I was about to say and made a decision.

"To be" scared, "or not to be."

I walked to the front of the room.

"To be" a prisoner, "or not to be."

I turned around to face my teacher and friends. I can do this, just like I practiced. I can do this, just like I've done before.

I stuttered, but kept going.

"To be" brave, "or not to be." To be bold.

I started to speak. My hands quivered. The words came out shaky at first. Then, I delivered them louder, stronger. I imagined myself saying the speech to my mom, grandma, and Mr. K. I stuttered, but kept going. I stayed focused and stood tall. Before I knew it, my speech was over. I smiled as everyone clapped for me.

They celebrated my reading just as they cheered everyone else's. But I had a special reason to feel good. I faced my fear. I knew I'd have other battles with stuttering, but I won that day.

I finally found my voice.

— Kelly Starling Lyons —
Chicken Soup for the Soul: Teens Talk High School

Kelly had a stutter. What do you want to overcome?

_____

_____

Kelly practiced her speech over and over. What can you do about your particular challenge?

_____

_____

Kelly ended up stuttering but kept going anyway, and everyone clapped. Does that help you feel better about your own challenge?

_____

_____

To Be King

Be content with what you have; rejoice in
the way things are. When you realize there
is nothing lacking, the whole world
belongs to you.
~Lao Tzu

As I took my seat at the pep rally, I looked around the packed gymnasium and thought this was completely and absolutely ridiculous. The four other boys sitting with me were the captains of the football, basketball, soccer and track teams. They were also voted best dressed, most athletic and best looking during the senior superlatives. I, on the other hand, was none of those things. I ran cross-country and, while I always tried hard, I wasn't really good. I could also guarantee that I wasn't going to get any votes for best looking or best dressed anytime soon. I wondered if this was all some sort of weird joke, because I could not comprehend what I was doing sitting with them.

During the ceremony, my mind wandered and I thought back to the last six months. I know that high school students tend to overdramatize things, but I honestly can say that those six months had more highs and lows than most high school students experience in such a short time.

It all started in April when I and three other boys were selected to represent our high school at a national conference on politics in Washington, D.C. While the trip was fun, I had a hard time connecting with people and by the end of the week felt pretty lonely. A few weeks later I ran for the only thing I had ever wanted in school — Student Government President. It was a very close election, but when it was over, I had lost. That night was brutal as I spent hours on the phone with, of all people, my chemistry teacher. I wondered if there was something else I could have done, and he tried his best to reassure me. But still it hurt.

Things got better a few weeks after that when I and three of my classmates were chosen to represent the school at Boys State, a leadership program intended to bring the best and the brightest male students together. That week, though, was a disaster. I was ridiculed by almost all the other boys except for my own classmates. In a blatant attempt to ridicule me further, I was nominated for the position of State Treasurer. I knew it was only to give my tormentors another chance to poke fun at me, as I'd have to speak to the whole group of a few hundred students.

I gave a speech where I called them out on their behavior.

So with the help of a friend from school on the trip, I gave a speech where I called them out on their behavior and expressed my disgust at what the supposed best and brightest had done. Shockingly, the speech was almost unanimously well received. I received a standing ovation, and the award for best delegate.

The summer passed by fairly uneventfully, until August when I was T-boned while driving my father to the airport. I was lucky to escape with minor injuries.

Through all of these events, I grappled with a choice. I had been presented with an opportunity to change myself, but it was not going to be easy. To put it bluntly, I'm short. I stand barely five feet tall, and have been since I was probably thirteen years old. When I was younger it wasn't that big a deal. But as I went through my teenage years, I stopped growing while everyone else continued to do so. The choice was to undergo a complex surgery. It involved breaking both my legs and then inserting pins between them to lengthen the bones. If it sounds painful, that is because it is. I would need to take a year off to deal with the medical issues. During those past six months, I wondered if things would have been easier if I were taller. Would I have won the election? Would I have not spent a week being ridiculed by a couple hundred teenage boys? Would that have somehow prevented the accident?

> I wondered if things would have been easier if I were taller.

I snapped out of my funk and my mind stopped wandering when I heard my name called. I needed to run one of the pep rally contests. As I walked to the microphone, I searched the crowd for a particular young lady. I had fallen for her and was hoping she would go to the senior prom with me in June, assuming I'd get the nerve to even ask her. Dating for me was nonexistent. While I had some good close friends, I was never part of the "popular" crowd and spent many nights at home. The school had a semi-formal dance every year in which the girls ask the boys, and I had never been asked to go with someone, even as a group thing. I often wondered if girls would be more interested if I were taller.

The contest was over and I went back to my seat. Thankfully, this whole ceremony would soon be over. A short time later, I heard a shout from the crowd and the girl sitting next to me elbowed me and whispered, "Stand up, we won!" For a second I didn't move, but as the throng of people came to congratulate us, I realized what had happened. Somehow, I had been elected Homecoming King. The rest of the afternoon was a blur until I got home and my chemistry teacher was on the phone. He remembered our conversation from that past May when, in tears, I had asked him if I would have won the election if I were taller. This afternoon, he wanted to make sure that I finally realized none of that mattered.

It has been twenty-one years since that day. I'll never really know why the students voted the way they did. But to each of them that did, I owe a big thank you. They taught me that the biggest obstacle I needed to overcome wasn't being short. It was being okay with who I was. And that if they were okay with it, then I should be too.

We all have our strengths and our weaknesses. For many of us, the challenge is seeing the good in ourselves. I had been

> **I had been myself during high school and that had been enough.**

myself during high school and that had been enough. My classmates saved me from choosing an unnecessary and painful surgery. I opted not to have the surgery and graduated on time with my classmates. When the senior superlatives came out, I didn't get best dressed or best looking. But I got something just as good: friendliest. I also did ask that particular young lady to the prom and she accepted.

— Rajkumar Thangavelu —
Chicken Soup for the Soul: Find Your Inner Strength

Chapter 6

COUNT YOUR BLESSINGS

The Lucky One

The happiest moments of my life have been the few which I have passed at home in the bosom of my family.
—Thomas Jefferson

Megan Williams. The most popular girl at Northlake High. She was head cheerleader, Prom Queen, Student Body President and a straight-A student. She was so perfect that it made me want to dislike her, but I couldn't. Because the truth was that Megan was a really nice person.

When I passed her in the hallway at school, she always smiled at me but rarely stopped to talk. Megan was friendly with everyone, but her true friends were all in the popular crowd. And I wasn't exactly hanging with them.

But when I saw Megan at the drugstore one Saturday morning, she was chatty and all smiles. "Hi, Diane," she said. "How are you?"

I smiled back. "I'm doing great. How about you?"

"I'm good, but kinda tired. I had to cheer last night."

"Oh, yeah, I forgot about the game. Did our team win?"

She nodded. "You weren't there?"

I shrugged. "I don't go to a lot of school stuff."

"Oh, you should. It's really fun."

I shrugged again and said nothing. But in my head, I thought, "Well, sure, everything is fun if you're Megan Williams."

I glanced at Megan's cart and spotted several bottles of hair conditioner. Megan's hair was gorgeous and I instantly decided to switch brands.

"Well, I guess I'll see you later," Megan said, starting to push her cart down the aisle. "Have a fun weekend."

"Yeah, you too," I said, already knowing that she would.

I grabbed a bottle of Megan's brand of conditioner and the other things I needed and then went through the checkout line. Megan got behind me in line.

I waved awkwardly and said, "Hi again."

She smiled and waved back.

I paid for my stuff and went out to my car, an old hatchback. It was my brother's car, which was passed down to me when he went away to college. It was a real junker, but it was mine.

I put my stuff in the back and was climbing into the car when I heard someone calling my name. It was Megan. "Diane, your car — it's so cute!"

"You think my car is cute?"

"Well, not the car itself, but the windows. That's really sweet."

I nodded and glanced at my car windows. I'd forgotten about the car's homemade decorations. On one window were the words, "I love you," written in wipe-off marker. Another window said, "You are beautiful," and a third read, "I believe in you."

"That's so nice," Megan said, "but I didn't know you had a boyfriend."

"Oh, I don't," I said, suddenly ashamed of my cute car windows.

"Then who wrote on your car?"

"Well, um, my dad did," I answered quietly.

> "Your dad took the time to write on your car windows, just to, you know, make you feel good?"

"Your dad did that? Your dad took the time to write on your car windows, just to, you know, make you feel good?"

I nodded, wishing like crazy I'd thought quickly enough to make up an imaginary boyfriend from another school. But I'd told the truth, which was beyond embarrassing.

I looked at Megan and realized she had tears in her eyes. "My dad would never do that for me," she muttered. "You are so lucky."

My mouth dropped open. Megan Williams thought I was lucky?

"I bet your mom's great too, right?"

I nodded. "Yeah, I guess. She stays at home with my little brother and sister. She bakes cookies and helps me with my homework and stuff."

Megan sighed. "I'd give anything to have a family like that."

"But you have everything," I said. "A perfect life."

She shook her head. "Not really. Not in the ways that matter."

After that, Megan always stopped to talk with me in the hallway. We even started hanging out outside of school. I'd offer to meet her at McDonald's or Subway, but she always wanted to come to my house. She seemed to love talking with my parents over a homemade dinner and playing board games with my family.

It was totally uncool, but it was what Megan wanted to do. I didn't understand why, but I didn't care. I'd always wanted to be friends with someone like Megan. I thought hanging out with her would make me popular and that would make me happy.

But just being Megan's friend made me happy. The other stuff didn't matter anymore.

Months later, Megan and I were talking about the day my dad wrote on my car windows. "I was so jealous of you," she admitted. "People think I have this great life, but I have struggles too."

I nodded because now that we were friends, I knew the truth about Megan's life.

> **"People think I have this great life, but I have struggles too."**

"But you know what? I decided something that day," she said. "Rather than feel bad that I don't have a dad that would do something like that for me, I decided to hang out with your family." She looked at me, determination in her eyes. "Someday when I'm married, I'm going to have a family like yours. My kids are going to feel so loved."

I realized in that moment that many things in this life are beyond our control. We can't change the family we were born into. Whether they're terrific or completely dysfunctional, we can only do our best to learn from what we're given.

Megan did that. And she showed me that I was the lucky one after all.

— Diane Stark —
Chicken Soup for the Soul: Just for Teenagers

Please Don't Leave

*The best way to find yourself is to lose
yourself in the service of others.*
—Mahatma Gandhi

I'd done it before, and so I had no reason to believe that this time would be any different. I was sure that when I returned home from my mission trip, as always, I'd bring back nothing more than some mud on my boots, a hole or two in my jeans and, of course, a lot of great memories. Little did I know that this time it was going to be different.

The summer before my high school graduation, I went to West Virginia with others from my church as members of the Appalachia Service Project. Our goals included refurbishing the homes of those in need, and where we were heading, there was no shortage of need. Along with volunteers from several other churches, we arrived at our destination much like an invading army in miniature, and we arrived ready to do battle. The tools we brought from home would serve as our weapons as we prepared to wage war against an all-too-familiar

> **Our mission was to make the homes of those we served warmer, safer and drier.**

enemy — substandard living conditions. Our mission was to make the homes of those we served warmer, safer and drier, and with only five days to accomplish as much as we could, we were anxious to get started.

My group was assigned the task of rebuilding sections of a home that had been damaged by fire. No sooner had we parked on the home's dirt driveway than we saw an excited little girl, no more than six years old, standing in the doorway of the family's temporary trailer home. Shoeless and wearing dirty clothes and the biggest smile I'd ever seen, she yelled, "Ma, Ma, they really came!" I didn't know it then, but her name was Dakota, and four more days would pass before she'd say another word near me.

Behind Dakota was a woman in a wheelchair — her grandmother, we'd soon learn. I also discovered that my job that week would be to help convert a fire-damaged dining room into a bedroom for this little girl. After meeting several more family members, we got down to the business of making a difference in their lives.

Grabbing our tools, we went to work. Walls were torn down and replaced. Hammers and nails, saws and electric screw guns, drywall prepping and painting — we moved at a fast pace. Over the following days, I noticed Dakota peeking at us every now and then as we worked. A few times, I tried talking with her, but she remained shy and aloof, always fluttering around us like a tiny butterfly but keeping to herself.

By our fifth and final day, however, this was about to change.

Before I went to work on her home on that last morning, I spoke for a moment or two with the grandmother. I was especially pleased when she told me how much Dakota loved her new room — so much, in fact, that she'd begged to sleep in it the previous night, even though it wasn't quite ready. As we talked, I noticed something I hadn't seen before — Dakota was hiding behind her grandmother. Cautiously, she stepped into view, and I could see that just like her clothes, her face was still dirty. But no amount of soil could hide those bright blue eyes and big smile. She was simply adorable. I wanted so much to hug her, but respecting her shyness, I kept my distance.

Slowly, she began walking toward me. It wasn't until she was just inches away that I noticed the folded piece of paper in her tiny hand. Silently, she reached up and handed it to me. Once unfolded, I looked at the drawing she'd made with her broken crayons on the back of an old coloring book cover. It was of two girls — one much taller than the other — and they were holding hands. She told me it was supposed to be me and her, and scrawled on the bottom of the paper were three little words that instantly broke my heart: *Please don't leave.* Now almost in tears, I surrendered to the impulse that I'd suppressed only moments before — I bent down and hugged her. She hugged me, too. And for the longest time, neither one of us could let go.

By early afternoon, we finished Dakota's bedroom, and so

> **I began to realize how frivolous various aspects of my own life were.**

I gladly used the rare free time to get to know my newest friend. Sitting under a tree away from the others, we shared a few apples while she told me about her life in the hollow. As I listened to her stories about the struggles she and her family endured daily, I began to realize how frivolous various aspects of my own life were.

Suddenly, things like deciding what to wear on a Friday night or which wannabe celebrity was starring in the latest reality television series seemed trivial. I refocused on my friends, family and faith, all because of one special little girl living in the mountains of West Virginia.

I left for home early the next morning. I was returning with muddy boots and holes in my jeans. But because of Dakota, I brought back something else, too — a greater appreciation for all of the blessings of my life. I'll never forget that barefoot little butterfly with the big smile and dirty face. I pray that she'll never forget me either.

— Tracy Rusiniak —
Chicken Soup for the Soul: My Kind of America

Tracy realized that many of the things she cared about were "frivolous." When you think about what other people don't have, what should you stop focusing on in your own life?

Three unimportant things in my life are:

1. _____

2. _____

3. _____

A Mother When I Needed One

You cannot save people.
You can only love them.
~Anaïs Nin

It was November 7, 2014, my eighth grade year. My teacher had asked me to come in after school. I didn't know why. I certainly didn't think she knew about my suicide plans.

I had been planning to kill myself on November 11th for months. I remember looking at the calendar and choosing the date. It was shortly after my mother's birthday, but before the holidays. It was when it would all stop—all of the pain, all of life.

Normally, teachers called me in after school to ask if they could keep my papers, but not about this. Most teachers just saw my good grades, and I suppose to most of them that meant I must be okay.

However, that day, I stayed after school with my teacher

for four hours, revealing everything that had led up to this point in my life: the divorce, the abuse, and the escape.

I watched my strong, brave teacher cry as she tried so hard to crack my tough shell. She wouldn't leave me until I was safe, and because of that, I owe her my life.

> I watched my strong, brave teacher cry as she tried so hard to crack my tough shell.

Throughout the rest of the school year, we met once a week. During a rocky period in my life, she was there for me when no one else was, and that's all I needed: someone who would listen, someone who would care, someone who would love me.

She was the best counselor anyone could ever ask for, the best friend I never had, and the best mother when I didn't have one.

The end of the year came, and I constructed a quote with my newly gained wisdom from her. With graphite handy, I sketched the words into unbreakable tree branches amongst blooming flower buds.

Every now and again, I still go to visit her, and there, high on her wall, it hangs in a black photo frame: "Beautiful is the one who's constant in making others' lives beautiful."

And she is beautiful.

— Brie Dalliant, age 16 —
Chicken Soup for the Soul: Inspiration for Teachers

The Greatest Blessing

*We should certainly count our blessings,
but we should also make
our blessings count.*
-Neil A. Maxwell

I was raised by a single mother who often worked several jobs just to make ends meet. When I was fifteen, she started dating the man who is now my stepfather, and things began to get easier financially. There was no longer a question as to whether she'd be able to afford groceries for the week.

The following spring, when I was sixteen, a new family began attending our church. The wife, Melissa, quickly befriended my mom, and the children, though younger than I, became my pals. They lived within walking distance from us, and once school let out for the summer, I would trek over to their house to watch Disney movies while my mom was at work.

One afternoon, I was at their house during lunchtime, and

they were gracious enough to include me in the meal. Their daughter, ten at the time, requested a glass of milk with her food. Melissa stated, "We're out of milk, and we don't have any more money for groceries this week." She suddenly realized I was present and explained with a defeated look, "Money has been really tight."

> "We're out of milk, and we don't have any more money for groceries this week."

The family had recently moved to Central Pennsylvania from California because Melissa had been offered a good job. The position hadn't worked out, and her husband had to take the first job he could find. They had uprooted their children and moved across the country, leaving behind family and friends, only to end up in a bind. I thought about our own circumstances just a year earlier.

Later, I trudged home with a heavy heart as I reflected on their hardship. I told my Mom about the rough time Melissa and her family were experiencing. "Do you think we could help them?" I asked. In response, she immediately flung open the cupboard doors and started pulling out food. We ransacked each cabinet, grabbing bag after bag, can after can — cereal, peanut butter, spaghetti sauce, and more. Then we tackled the canning shelf where Mom's precious homemade goods were stored. We found a sizable box and packed it full. Then off we went to the grocery store where we picked up perishables such as milk and eggs. We drove to our friends' house, made our way to the door with our box and bags, and knocked eagerly.

When they opened the door, all four of them were there, clearly surprised by our visit. As we stepped inside the kitchen,

> I trudged home with a heavy heart as I reflected on their hardship.

their eyes found the box, and the parents' jaws dropped. Handing the items over to them, Mom said, "We just wanted to bless you." They were speechless. Melissa then grasped Mom in a tight embrace and started to sob. Tears began to roll down my mother's face as she held onto her friend, feeling her pain, fear and frustration, understanding how devastating it can be to struggle to provide for your family. I felt my eyes moisten and throat tighten with emotion as I watched my mother. Then I looked over at the children. Their son was beaming, and their daughter was sniffing away tears.

My gaze shifted back to my mom, and I was proud to be the daughter of this incredible woman. She was the one who had worked so hard to pay for the groceries that she didn't hesitate to give to those in need. Because of her, we were able to share this amazing experience. What a great example she set for me that day! Though our intentions were to bless our friends, thirteen years later I still feel like I'm the one who received the greatest blessing: one of my most cherished memories with my mom.

— Savannah D. Cassel —
Chicken Soup for the Soul: My Amazing Mom

GIVE

LIVE

LOVE

Chicken Soup for the Soul

A Heart Full of Memories

*I am not the same, having seen the moon
shine on the other side of the world.*
~Mary Anne Radmacher

"There is no way I can live out of a suitcase!" I thought as we packed up our home in Venice, Italy. At fourteen years old, I couldn't imagine leaving my friends, school, and all my "stuff" behind to travel the world full-time with my family.

At the time, we were all going in different directions — my sister and I were stressed and focused on school and were rarely home and my parents were focused on work. I was focused on my friends, the latest gadget, and the current fashions — always wanting

> I couldn't imagine leaving my friends, school, and all my "stuff" behind to travel the world full-time.

to buy new clothes that "fit in." Between doing my homework, texting, seeing my friends, and going to my activities, I rarely had time to spend with my family. It felt like we never saw each other even though we lived under the same roof.

That was when my mom had the idea of dropping everything to travel the world and reconnect as a family. One day she sat us down at the kitchen table and proposed the idea, which at the time seemed so crazy. Although I absolutely loved the idea of traveling the world freely, I couldn't imagine leaving my life behind. After several months of planning, packing, and saying goodbye to our old lives, off we went to explore the world with no end date in sight!

That was over two years, thirty-eight countries, and four continents ago! During that time, we have realized how little we really need to be happy. We have learned how the most important moments in life aren't when we get new gifts or things, but when we live happy moments with our family and friends. We know now that experiences are the best treasures.

We have realized how little we really need to be happy.

As we travel, we barely carry anything with us except the essential things like clothes, a laptop, notebooks, and toiletries. We each carry a backpack and all five of us share two suitcases for clothes. After buying new trinkets or new clothes, we give some of our old outfits away to people in need and it makes us so happy to be able to give back wherever we can.

The small amount of baggage we have makes it easy to

travel from country to country on planes, trains, buses, ferries, tuk tuks, etc. By traveling so light, we get to do more with less. We are free to explore countries easily and move around as much as we like. Many times we even make spontaneous travel plans and it is so easy to pack up our stuff and go!

At the beginning, it was difficult for us to get used to never having a closet, constantly changing hotel rooms, and never fully unpacking before we were back on the road. But over time we have learned to appreciate the value of having less — the freedom to live for experiences and the joy of traveling "light" in mind, body, and spirit.

Meeting new people and getting to know their cultures has been the best part of traveling for me. Instead of focusing on things, we love to focus on the people and connect with them. Wherever we go, we try to make as many friends as we can and feel like we have "family" in countries all over the world!

Many of the wonderful new friends we have made on our journey have opened our eyes to how lucky we are. We have met families in many parts of the world who live in small homes with no running water or on the streets escaping war and violence, yet they always have huge smiles and are willing to share with us.

Without all the distractions that we used to have, we have become connected as a family! I can honestly say that travel is the best way for a family to become close again, since it takes away all the distractions and reminds us of what is really important. We now know that experiences and memories are the most valuable things in life and that they can only be acquired when we let go of our need for possessions and focus on what really matters in life — enjoying our lives each day with the people we love.

So I would now say to my fourteen-year-old self, "I will gladly give up a home full of stuff to live out of a suitcase with a heart full of memories!"

— Kaitlin Murray, age 17 —
Chicken Soup for the Soul: The Joy of Less

Chapter 7

TREASURE YOUR FAMILY

Just Twenty Hours

*I don't believe an accident of birth makes
people sisters or brothers... Sisterhood
and brotherhood is a condition people
have to work at.*
~Maya Angelou

Freshman year of college. World History class. My professor has just dropped a bombshell on the class. Thirty percent of our final grade will be based on an assignment that is going to take, at minimum, twenty hours to complete. The assignment? Community service.

"We are all part of a community. Whether or not a community succeeds is largely dependent on how citizens treat each other. So go out into your communities — get involved, but do it in a way that you don't get paid. Making cookies and taking them to your neighbor doesn't count. It has to be something that is actually going to take some time, and I can assure you there are plenty of ways to help out in your community. It is my belief that this assignment will change your life. It is only for twenty hours, but you might be surprised what can happen in those twenty hours."

Some people in my class grumbled. I wasn't particularly irritated by the assignment, but I was trying to figure out how I would find the time. I was going to school only part-time because I was working full-time to pay for college. I eventually just shrugged my shoulders and thought, "I'm just going to have to make it work."

> It is my belief that this assignment will change your life.

After doing some research, I found an after-school tutoring program for kids held in a former elementary school. I filled out my paperwork, paid the fee for a background check, and a week later got a phone call saying that I had been paired with a fourth-grade boy named Steven.

He was small for his age, wore glasses and was a Harry Potter fan. He was a little on the quiet side for the first few weeks, but it was obvious he was a very bright boy. He didn't need a tutor as much as he needed a friend. I don't think he was bullied at school or anything like that; it seemed that his classmates mostly ignored him.

We met twice a week for two hours, so it only took me five weeks to complete the necessary hours for my class. When I started, I only intended to complete the required hours for my assignment. But when the hours were done, I realized how small a sacrifice it had been for me to tutor Steven. I still had sufficient time to do my schoolwork, my full-time job, and even spend time with family and friends. But most importantly, I liked

Steven. And I could tell that he had already grown attached to me. There was no way I was going to back out on that kid.

Most days, Steven finished his homework in half an hour if he even had any. That meant we could do other things. We played *Jenga* and air hockey. He mentioned he was a *Star Wars* fan, so I brought my sister's *Star Wars Monopoly* game so that we could practice math skills and play a nerdy game at the same time. We read the fourth *Harry Potter* book together and wondered what was going to happen in the final three and argued over whether or not Snape was a bad guy. In the winter, we had snowball fights. When the second *Star Wars* movie came out, I got permission from his grandparents to take him to the movie. We were both totally disappointed by it, but

He didn't need a tutor as much as he needed a friend.

we still had fun. I got him an R2-D2 keychain. He called me a dork, but that keychain was quickly attached to the zipper on his backpack.

As the end of the school year approached, Steven started to get a little depressed. I finally asked him one day what was wrong. He said, "I don't want the school year to end."

"But, Steven, I thought you didn't like school." He had told me on numerous occasions that he didn't.

"I don't."

"Then why don't you want the school year to end?"

He was quiet for a second, and then said, "Because when the school year is over, I won't see you anymore. We won't come here and you will forget all about me."

I felt like crying. "Steven, I will never forget you."

"But we still won't get to see each other like we do."

"No, we won't." I had signed an agreement stating that at the end of the school year I wouldn't seek to have a relationship with the child I tutored. It hadn't seemed like a big deal nine months before and I understood the reasons behind it. But now that the school year was coming to a close, I realized it really did stink that I wasn't going to be able to hang out with this awesome young man anymore. He had become so much more than just a kid I spent time with to fulfill a class requirement. He was like a little brother. "I'm going to miss you, too, Steven, but I promise I will never, ever forget you." I don't think I really made him feel any better, but I knew that I couldn't lie to him and say that we were still going to see each other on a regular basis.

We were supposed to have one last day together, but on that day, the supervisor of the tutoring program called to tell me that he had been offered a new job and was leaving, so never mind, no tutoring today. I called Steven to tell him the news and he was heartbroken. "But I got you a present!" So I got on the phone with his grandpa and he told me to come over so that Steven could say goodbye.

I ended up staying for about an hour. He had gotten me a teddy bear with a pink bow tied around its neck. I handed him paperback copies of the first two *Harry Potter* books. Then Steven gave me a school picture and a note. The note read, "I will never forget you. You were my best friend this year. I will remember you always." It was probably the most heartfelt note that I have ever received.

It took me some time to get used to not heading over to that old elementary school and seeing that sweet, smiling boy waiting for me. But then I realized I had a young boy in my life about the same age, with a sweet smile of his own, a boy I didn't see enough: my own brother.

I had been so busy being an adult that I really didn't pay him any attention at all. And then I realized I hadn't been spending any time with my younger sister, either. I had a brother and a sister who I loved and cared about, but when I actually took the time to think about it, I realized I wasn't really friends with them. Other than the obligatory nightly dinner routine and going to their various school functions, I didn't spend any time with them. I had just spent nine months getting to know a kid, but I couldn't say the same thing about my own brother and sister.

> I had just spent nine months getting to know a kid, but I couldn't say the same thing about my own brother and sister.

It was time to change that. I started going on weekly dates with my brother, even letting him pick what we did. Sometimes that meant playing *Pokémon* games, something I abhorred, but the look of excitement on my brother's face made it worth it. I started inviting my sister to do things with my friends and me. Sure enough, in less than a year my siblings became much more than just my siblings. They are my best friends. I don't know if I would have ever become as close to them as I am now if it hadn't been for that assignment from my history professor.

I still think about Steven. He's at least twenty years old now. I wonder what he's up to. I wonder if he even remembers me. But mostly I am grateful that even though we didn't get to continue our friendship, it was because of that friendship that I realized I was missing out on having relationships with my siblings. My professor was right: A lot can happen in just twenty hours.

— Nicole Webster —
Chicken Soup for the Soul: Volunteering & Giving Back

Family
First

Pictures Don't Lie

Don't handicap your children by
making their lives easy.
–Robert A. Heinlein

The first time I ever got drunk my parents took pictures of me throwing up and passed out on my bed. When they gave me one of those pictures the next day, I was furious. I just grabbed it and slammed my way out of the kitchen. I did not want to talk about it and I ripped that picture to shreds. I didn't know there were several more even worse than that one.

For the next few mornings, there was a different picture next to my plate. "When you're ready to talk about it, we're ready to listen," my mom said. By the time the last picture showed up, I was ready to talk about it.

> "When you're ready to talk about it, we're ready to listen," my mom said.

This all started when Mike Emery invited me to his birthday party. I was so excited. He was turning fourteen and had worked out a theme to have fourteen people, seven girls and seven boys. I could not wait to get on my cell and find out if Gayle, my best friend, had also gotten an invitation. Gayle and I have been best friends since third grade and our birthdays are only three days apart. She and her brother Steve had lived with their mom since her parents' divorce, and Gayle's mom had already let her go to a couple of parties before this one.

My mom and dad are pretty strict, especially my dad. They finally agreed to let me go, mostly because Mike's parents would be around during the party. Mom and Dad laid down some rules about when I had to be home. Really lame rules, in my opinion, but I was ready to agree to anything.

Gayle and I must have changed our minds a hundred times about what to wear. We were going to go in jeans until Mike texted us to "look pretty." I decided to wear my favorite yellow dress that made my tan really look good. Dad bought the dress for me a few months before for my cousin's wedding. It was definitely the most expensive dress I had ever owned.

You should have seen their expressions when I got dressed and walked into the living room with my hair piled up on my head in a way I had never done before. I used a lot of hairspray and some gold sparkles and, frankly, I had never looked so hot. My parents just stared at me and, finally, Mom said, "Honey, you are so beautiful!" Dad stared at me a few minutes; then he went for the camera, insisting on taking pictures.

Gayle's mom dropped us off at the party and her brother,

Steve, agreed to pick us up at 11:30 and drop us off at home. Steve is eighteen and loves any excuse to drive his mom's Mustang.

As soon as we got to Mike's house, I started feeling really nervous. I'm not sure why. I knew most of the people there, but I just wasn't used to being all dressed up and wished I felt as good as they said I looked. The dining room table had a big bowl on it full of pink punch, with sliced peaches floating on top. There was plenty of food on the table, but nobody was eating any of it. I was kind of surprised that I hadn't seen Mike's parents around after the party got started, but someone said they were in the den watching TV. Mike put on some good music, but nobody was dancing. In fact, the girls hung out at one end of the room and the guys at the other, just kind of pushing each other around and acting like jerks. I kept flashing looks at Gayle, but she didn't catch on to how uncomfortable I was feeling.

That's when I saw Mike pour a bottle of vodka into the punch. I heard him say to nobody in particular, "We've gotta get this show on the road." Another boy said, "Yeah Mike, this party really sucks. Do it."

I have no clue how I got home.

I remember going to the table with an empty glass in my hand and asking Mike to fill it up. Then I drank it fast, all at once, and asked for more. I remember my eyes doing strange things and the room going around and around. That's about all I remember. I have no clue how I got home.

When I saw that first picture, I felt sick all over again.

There I was, hurling all over my dress, with my hair all stringy and matted. The ones of me passed out on my bed made me look dead. It scared me to look at those photos. After ripping up that first one, I did not even want to touch the others.

Of course, my parents were totally upset and they called Mike's mom and dad the day after the party. They came right over, with Mike, and did a lot of apologizing. I had to stand there and it was so embarrassing. All I could say was, "It's not Mike's fault." What I really wanted to do was just go to bed and be left alone.

For that whole weekend, my head ached, my eyes hurt, and I did not want to talk to anyone, including Gayle. My mom kept looking at me with this sad expression on her face. And my dad was definitely very angry. Mostly what they kept saying was, "When you want to talk about it, let us know."

I'm not sure when I decided it was time to talk about it. I think it was the last day of pictures when they put the "before" ones down next to the "after" ones. You would not believe it was the same person. I couldn't believe it. My parents did not have to tell me how ugly I looked, bombed out of my mind. I could see for myself.

Maybe if my dad had not taken all those pictures, I would never have known what I looked like when I got drunk... and maybe I never would

> Maybe if my dad had not taken all those pictures, I would never have known what I looked like when I got drunk.

have talked to them about it. Not that I had much to say. What

I did tell them was this: "I lost a couple of hours of my life last weekend. I swear it won't happen again."

And it hasn't.

— Becca Johnson —
Chicken Soup for the Soul: Just for Teenagers

She Understood

A grandma is warm hugs and sweet
memories. She remembers all of your
accomplishments and forgets
all of your mistakes.
~Barbara Cage

I had been trying to have this conversation with my grandmother for a long time. Four months. Four months since I left the harsh streets of Brooklyn and the unaccepting, neglectful home of my father. Four months since my last period. I was fourteen years old and I didn't know much about anything, but I knew enough to realize I was pregnant.

I thought that maybe if I just forgot what happened, it would go away. I thought that maybe my belly would stop growing. That maybe I would stop throwing up and be able to eat again.

I had no idea how my grandmother would react. She had always been so loving when I was a young child. There were eleven of us grandchildren at the time but I felt like I had always been her favorite.

She had become a mother at the age of fifteen and I knew she always wanted so much more for me. So when I started to tell her, the words wouldn't come out. All I could do was cry. I ran from the small living room of the two-bedroom trailer that housed seven people, through the screen door and out on to the wooden front porch. It was an October night in North Carolina. It was cold out. Cold, now that was something I was used to.

I stood there crying and shaking. I stared out into the black sky; the stars looked blurred through my tears. I heard

"Are you pregnant, honey?"

the screen door creak open behind me. My grandmother stood beside me and placed her hand on my shoulder. She looked down at my bare feet, my toes purple from the chill of the night air, and asked, "Are you pregnant, honey?"

My anguish and terror spilled out in sobs as I muttered, "yes" over and over again. When I found enough courage to look into my grandmother's face, her brown eyes were glowing with warmth. She was smiling. She took my hand and guided me back inside. "You certainly can't be out in this cold with no shoes on your feet, dear. How about I run you a bath?"

My fears all melted away in that bath. It was the most peaceful place I had ever found myself. Afterward, my grandmother wrapped me inside her bathrobe. I had always loved that robe. Grandmother would wear it in the early mornings as she cooked breakfast and read the newspaper. I am not sure of the material, but it was fabulously soft.

It felt as though I was wrapped in warm clouds. I rubbed my arms, hugging myself, and began to look deep into the baby pink fabric of the robe. I was studying it so closely and for the first time since I realized the truth of my situation, I had a pleasant thought. I was thinking about what color my baby would wear.

My grandmother knew what I was thinking. She smiled and said, "Maybe we'll have us a baby girl."

I smiled back. "Maybe." That night my grandmother told me stories of pregnancy and birth. We laughed, we planned, and we figured out what my next steps should be. We talked about everything from prenatal vitamins to college funds for the baby. My grandmother told me the story of my birth and the first time she saw me in the bassinet through the glass window in the nursery. I had heard that story many times before, but tonight it was even more special.

> We laughed, we planned, and we figured out what my next steps should be.

I have often been told that being a parent does not come with a book of instructions. Well, for those of us who are lucky, we can find many answers in the words and actions of the women who came before us.

That October night in North Carolina was a pivotal moment that shaped my future. Grandmother's strength, acceptance, and guidance in that moment have always served as a motivating force in my life. There is nothing quite like a mother's love, except perhaps for one thing: the love of a grandmother.

— Patricia Dublin —
Chicken Soup for the Soul: Best Mom Ever!

The Driving Lesson

A well-balanced person is one who finds both sides of an issue laughable.
~Herbert Procknow

A t sixteen, I possessed something every teenager dreams of... a learner's permit. But unlike most kids my age, I was terrified by the thought of navigating almost two tons of crushing steel.

"Do you want to drive home?" Mom asked when she picked me up from my after-school house-cleaning job.

I hesitated. "Really? Are you sure?"

Mom nodded with confidence. "You'll do fine."

"Okay." I hopped into the driver's seat of our Ford Galaxie 500.

"You've got plenty of room to back up," she said while I maneuvered in Mrs. Carlson's driveway.

The car bumped over potholes down the long dirt drive. When we reached the county road, I stopped. "Now, look both ways," Mom instructed. "Turn your wheel to the left. Give it some gas, but take it slow. We're not in any hurry."

I pulled onto the narrow two-lane road. We rolled along fine until a pickup truck barreled up behind us. Mom stiffened her back and leaned forward. I glanced in the rearview mirror. I guess it didn't occur to the man driving the blue rust bucket to slow down as he crowded our bumper. When I failed to speed up, he blasted his horn. My fingers clenched the wheel.

Mom pointed. "You'd better turn into the next driveway and let this guy pass."

Before I reached the place where I needed to turn, the guy laid on his horn again. In a panic, Mom exclaimed. "Turn, turn here. I said turn!"

I could see I wasn't close enough to make the turn, but I did as instructed. I jerked the steering wheel with a hard crank to the right and our car plunged into the ditch alongside the road. My foot slammed down on the gas pedal, and the engine bellowed like an angry bull. Our old Galaxie flew airborne up the other side of the ditch and plowed through a fence.

Mom yelled, "Hit the brake!" We bounced in the seat as the car landed with a thud in the middle of a pasture.

My hands dropped from the steering wheel. For a moment, we sat silently. I took several deep breaths, afraid to look at my mom.

I expected a harsh scolding.

Finally, she asked, "Are you okay?"

"Yeah." I turned to face her. I expected a harsh scolding, but when our eyes met, we burst into hysterical laughter. We threw open the doors and climbed from the car. Still laughing, we leaned against the fenders to steady ourselves.

Two brown horses stopped munching grass in the adjoining field. They trotted over to the wire fence to observe the strange happenings. If horses have eyebrows, theirs were certainly raised. They tilted their heads and stared, mouths agape. Their funny expressions triggered more giggles.

"Excuse me," a man's voice interrupted. "Excuse me. Are you ladies okay?"

We spotted the blue pickup parked in the driveway and an older man hiking toward us, totally confused at what was so funny.

Mom quickly pulled herself to a more dignified pose. Still shaken, she staggered through tall clumps of grass toward the irritated truck driver. "Yes, we're fine. I was just giving my daughter a driving lesson."

"I'm so sorry," he said. "I would never have honked my horn if I'd known a teenager was behind the wheel."

He checked the car over and didn't see any damage. However, the tires had sunk into the soft ground, leaving us stranded.

"Well, I'm in a hurry. As long as you ladies are okay, I'll be on my way."

"Thank you for stopping to check on us," Mom said.

We watched him hop into his truck and drive off. "You'd think he might have offered us a ride," I said.

The property owner didn't answer the door when we knocked. Mom scribbled a note with our name and phone number and wrote we'd be back to claim the car and have the fence repaired. Then we walked to her friend Jeannie's house, which wasn't far.

> **I saw her as a person, not just my mother.**

After a cup of tea and a good chuckle, Jeanie drove us home.

When Dad arrived home from work that evening, the first words out of his mouth were, "Where's the car?"

Mom and I exchanged a knowing smile, sealing a new bond between us. She told Dad what happened and admitted being partly at fault for overreacting to the situation. For the first time in my life, I saw her as a person, not just my mother.

And, thanks to Mom, that was not my last driving lesson.

— Kathleen Kohler —
Chicken Soup for the Soul: The Empowered Woman

Meant to Be

Biology is the least of what makes
someone a mother.
~Oprah Winfrey

I was fourteen when I learned that my mom was not my "real" mom. She actually told me on the day of my fourteenth birthday, explaining that I was now old enough to know the truth.

Mom had been working at the local CVS pharmacy and it was her week to open up as part of the morning shift. It was before 7 a.m. when she discovered a shopping cart from the adjacent dollar store parked in the pharmacy's entrance.

Quietly sleeping in the cart was a newborn baby wrapped in a soiled blue blanket. Nobody was around; the parking lot was empty. She opened the store, turned off the alarm, and called the police. While she waited, she checked to be sure that the baby was dry and

> I was fourteen when I learned that my mom was not my "real" mom.

comfortable. She carried him around the store, holding him to her warm body.

The police and the child services person arrived together and insisted on taking the baby to the hospital. My mom went with them. Even though the authorities kept telling her that it was none of her concern, she stayed there for two days. She badgered the nurses, the police and the child services representative, whose job it was to care for the baby, for information and demanded updates on their success in finding the baby's mother. They would come to learn, as I have, that when my mom is on a mission nothing gets in her way.

My mom couldn't have kids of her own, and she and my dad had been approved for adoption. My appearance was a sign so strong that she was relentless in her conviction that I was sent to her by a higher power. Her sheer determination and total ignorance of the law somehow convinced a judge that she could keep me while the official paperwork for my adoption was completed.

> She was relentless in her conviction that I was sent to her by a higher power.

Knowing that she's not my birth mother hasn't changed anything. It has only made me more appreciative of her. She said I was welcome to try to find my biological mother if I wanted, but no one could find her when I was born so I think a search would be a waste of time.

I do find myself looking at my mom differently once in a while because it's hard to believe that she's *not* my birth mother. We both have blue eyes and blond hair, and she's often mistaken for my older sister because we look so much alike. Neither of us likes broccoli. We are both left-handed, we both whistle in tune, we both have perfect pitch, and we both play the piano. We laugh or cry at the same movies, and we often share the same dreams. I may have trouble finding a girlfriend because I'll compare them all to my mom, and they'll all fall short. I have several friends who have nothing in common with their biological parents; it's uncanny how similar I am to my adoptive ones.

Now it may be easy to explain all these similar traits as coincidence or parental influence — it's certainly not heredity — but I had to draw the line on wishful conjecture when I discovered that my mom was born with a slight deformity called a hammer toe on her left foot. You guessed it, I have one too, and it's the same toe on the same foot! Explain that if you can.

— Derek H. —
Chicken Soup for the Soul: Best Mom Ever!

A Father's Love

Any man can be a father. It takes
someone special to be a dad.
~Author Unknown

Sweat dripped its way down my forehead and into my eyes quicker than I could wipe it away. Attempting to conquer my cottonmouth, I spat onto the red clay near first base and swept over it with my cleats. It was hot. The dugout thermometer read 109 degrees, but the air was still and the humidity was rising from the previous night's rain.

This was it, the last out. One final play and the State Softball Championship was ours. The pressure was on. The bases were loaded, their leadoff hitter was at bat, and we were only two runs ahead.

I glanced towards the crowd, searching for familiar faces. Sure enough, I found my mom braving the heat to cheer me on. It was only a routine thought to wish my dad were here. The farm demanded his full attention, but I did not care. I was selfish, always resenting him for choosing his work over me.

Out of the pitcher's glove and into the catcher's. Strike one. Again, only this time she swung and missed, just under the pitch. I could taste the sweet victory on my tongue as the pitcher stepped onto the mound.

Her wind-up was perfect, flinging a fastball right down the center. The bat cracked from the impact. An in-field fly to third sent us all scrambling for our bases, ready to protect our title. I worried that she would not catch it. The yellow ball was hidden in the sun, and the glare was overwhelming. Treading circles around the bag, the third baseman shaded her eyes with her glove.

She caught it.

Euphoria swept over me. State Champs! A scream of delight caught in my throat as we stormed the mound, interrupted by a wave of tears when I looked back at the crowd. My mom was there, giving me a thumbs-up and smiling. I smiled back at her through blurry eyes.

We all received medals, plaques—the works—but I cannot remember any of it. I focused my thoughts on my dad, who was not there. I ran to my mom, begging for her cell phone. I had to tell my dad about the happiest day of my life, and rub in how he did not care enough to come and watch me play.

The phone rang twice, and then went to voicemail. My heart sank with disappointment, but I tried again anyway.

"Hello?" My dad answered, the sound of a combine shutting down

> I focused my thoughts on my dad, who was not there.

in the background.

"Dad!" I cried. "We won State!"

Silence.

"Dad?" I could hear him sobbing on the other end. "Are you — crying?"

"I'm just really happy for you, Meggie," he said. "And I'm sorry I couldn't be there."

An apology was all I needed. I hung up the phone feeling perfectly at ease, and I began to understand how it must feel to be a father. My resentment dissolved as I forgave him for never being there. He worked so I could play; it was as simple as that. My father loved me enough to let me experience life's happiest moments without him.

> I began to understand how it must feel to be a father.

That is a father's love.

— Megan Thurlow —

Chicken Soup for the Soul: Just for Teenagers

"He worked so
I could play."

Megan realized that parents have competing obligations.

Name three things you can forgive in your family.

1.

_____

2.

_____

3.

_____

LOOK TO THE FUTURE

Endings Can Be Beginnings

**Every story has an end but in life every
ending is just a new beginning.
~Uptown Girls**

I still clearly remember the night when my dad gathered our family in the living room. After nearly eleven months of unemployment, we could sense what this meant. Even though my dad usually had a way with words, he skirted around saying what we knew was coming. Finally, he said it: "I accepted a new job." And in turn, I had to accept my fate.

I blurted out the obvious question, "Where?" Before my father could finish saying "Austin, Texas," I had burst into tears, practically inconsolable. I would have to completely start

> I would have to completely start over, which was less than ideal for a sophomore in high school.

over, which was less than ideal for a sophomore in high school. My crying continued well into the night.

After that I was done. Not another tear fell.

Following that December night I became numb, withdrawing into myself in an attempt to make leaving seem painless. While my dad commuted back and forth between California and Texas, my sister and I were allowed to finish out the school year, leaving me with six months to sabotage my relationships with people who cared about me. As a result I felt detached, almost as though I was living a double life while I kept this secret from my friends and others around me. I was consumed with self-pity, questioning the purpose of engaging in the world around me since I knew I was leaving. However, somewhere along the way of counting down the days in anticipation of the end, I found myself counting down the days in anticipation of the beginning.

Suddenly I stopped feeling sorry for myself. I decided to take charge of my life and add some certainty to my unclear future. I diligently researched high schools and neighborhoods, and in return my parents gave me a say in where we would begin the search for our new home in the Austin area. Once we purchased our new house, I could see my future unfolding before me. With knowledge comes power. I did not have to become a victim of my circumstance, but instead a victor. I could take this clean slate and use it as an opportunity for self-improvement.

My self-improvement began by emulating confidence. My end goal was to become proactive and independent, which at the time seemed overwhelming. I knew the only way to achieve this was by taking baby steps, so I e-mailed the tennis coach at my new high school and inquired about trying out for the team. The seemingly simple e-mail soon turned into a conversation as he put my mind at ease, reassuring me that I was "coming to a great school and tennis community," and my prospective team was looking forward to having me.

The interaction could not have gone better. Little did I know that would set the course for my "new and improved" life. My coach had gone on to inform the team of my arrival. Within the week, I was communicating with a redheaded girl on the varsity team named Danielle who had reached out to me via Twitter. It dawned on me that the only things she knew about me came from an Instagram account and a horribly outdated Facebook profile. This was my chance to put my clean slate to use. I could assume the role of the confident girl I wanted to be. For the first time I felt like I was in control, because for so long I had let other people, whether friends or unacquainted peers, control me. This was my time.

> **For the first time I felt like I was in control.**

More than six months after my family packed up our cars and drove to what I had come to view as my promised land, I have never felt more "me." I successfully threw myself into everything I possibly could, enjoying the process of uncovering what I truly did and didn't like, not what my peers dictated I *should* like.

At my old school I would have never given math club a

second thought, even though I was fairly skilled in the sub-

> **I have never felt more "me."**

ject. However, it was a new school, a new me, and I decided to challenge myself and join Mu Alpha Theta, a mathematics honor society. Shocking as it may be, I actually enjoyed being a "mathlete," but even more shocking to me was the fact that no one teased me for my decision. It seemed as though everyone around me had already realized that they should "live and let live."

It was then that I realized the judgments I perceived from others were, in actuality, nonexistent. The perceived ridicule was purely something I allowed myself to fear, and moving gave me the freedom to see that I decide what shapes me. The courage and confidence I had sought had been there all along, simply waiting beneath my insecurities to finally surface when the time was right.

The night I learned I was going to move, the person I used to be evaporated with my last tears. The debilitating dread of what I thought was the end was replaced by anticipation for a new beginning. While every new beginning contains an element of fear, it also contains an element of promise.

— Brianna Mears —
Chicken Soup for the Soul: Time to Thrive

Mindfulness Matters

Mindfulness is a way of befriending ourselves and our experience.
~Jon Kabat-Zinn

My great-grandfather inspired me to make a positive difference in the world. He was a very mindful person, and he taught me about positive thinking. He used to say things like "Think well to be well," and "Every day, we have a new choice to make, so choose to be happy."

Most of all, Grandpa Jack was always kind. He believed that a smile is not just a smile. It's a road to peace, one that kids can learn in pre-kindergarten, and something that can change the world. And he taught me that if we smile, even if we don't feel like it, our bodies get a positive signal from our brains, and the smile comes true! Grandpa knew then what scientists have since proven: Smiling is contagious.

> **I believe that the key to ending violence is teaching kids to be mindful when they're young.**

When Grandpa Jack passed away, I wanted to honor him by teaching his messages of positivity, kindness, and happiness to other kids. I believe that the key to ending violence is teaching kids to be mindful when they're young. That's why I started the Wuf Shanti Children's Wellness Foundation, to teach kids to live a healthy and happy life, using his wisdom.

Wuf Shanti is a dog character that teaches mindfulness, social and emotional learning, kindness, and positivity to kids from three to ten years old. Wuf Shanti has produced seven books; a free mobile app with signature games; and 100 videos, which have run on local PBS stations, the Children's TV Network (the station in children's hospitals across the nation), Adventure to Learning (health and fitness video programming in 25,000 schools) and Kidoodle.TV (safe streaming network for kids).

In my Wuf Shanti dog costume, I traveled to schools and children's hospitals to visit the kids and share our message with them. When Wuf would walk into the hospitals and meet the kids, especially the kids who had cancer — many of them bald from treatment or hooked up to tubes — they'd forget all that for a few minutes. They would smile and run up to Wuf to hug him, dance, or give a high-five.

Parents would cry with joy at seeing their kids smiling and happy. It had an impact on me. I felt sad seeing them like this, but happy about how my being there was helping their lives, even for a few minutes. It made me realize how good my life is and how so many people need help to be happier.

One time, my little sister was crying, and I was able to share Grandpa Jack's message. I told her that she had a choice to make. She could choose to be upset about not getting what she wanted, or she could choose to be happy for what she did have. About five minutes later, I overheard her calming herself down by repeating "think well, be well," while tapping her fingers one at a time against her thumb, one of the exercises Wuf Shanti teaches. You don't realize how much of an impact you're making until you witness a five-year-old control her own temper tantrum and bring positivity back into her life.

> She could choose to be upset about not getting what she wanted, or she could choose to be happy for what she did have.

I've used my grandpa's teaching often. For example, when I became a teenager, I got self-conscious when some of my friends teased me about being a dog character. So, I did what Grandpa taught me to do: I laughed. They stop teasing you if they see it doesn't bother you.

And I took action by expanding our curriculum for older kids, ages eleven to seventeen (minus the dog character). My mission is to provide kids and teens with coping tools so they grow up less depressed and anxious. I want them to become happy, peace-loving adults who solve their problems in productive ways. I consider these techniques to be life skills. My goal is to get these mindful, social-and-emotional-learning programs into schools across the country as part of their core curriculums.

We live near Parkland, Florida and the tragic shooting that happened at Marjory Stoneman Douglas High School. That made me want to do even more, so I founded the Kids' Association for Mindfulness in Education for teens to collaborate and figure out ways to work together to make the world a better place. I also founded the international online Mindful Kids Peace Summit for middle schools and high schools. More than fifty subject-matter experts spoke about diversity, kindness, anti-bullying, communication, mindfulness, positivity, learning to interact with others, compassion, collaboration, positive psychology, and more.

> Sometimes, I find it hard to put down my phone and look up, but I force myself to do it.

Through working on all of this, I've learned that even when you feel like giving up (like when you see yet another shooting on the news), you have to work even harder. I've also learned that collaboration is key. We can't change the world alone. Even though I'm a mindful kid, I get sad or upset sometimes. Sometimes, I find it hard to put down my phone and look up, but I force myself to do it. I now tell people that if they can just practice mindfulness for five minutes every day, it can help them.

Science has proven that mindfulness helps us relax, stay

focused, do better in school and sports, stay healthy, heal faster, get along better with others, and live a happier life. There will always be stress in life that we'll have to deal with, so we need to stop thinking negatively and start focusing on the positive. We need to connect with each other and smile. "Think well to be well," as my grandpa would say. It can change our lives and change the world. It's a lesson that I take to heart every day.

— Adam Avin —
Chicken Soup for the Soul: Think Positive, Live Happy

Editor's note: You can watch Adam's TEDx Talk at https://www.tedxkc.org/adam-avin-kcyouth or on YouTube at https://youtu.be/2r6TWTqr8FM.

Food Should Be Fun

You do it with your own two hands, so
there's a sense of pride. You really do
forget all our problems, because you're
focusing on the food.
~Rachael Ray

I am not your average seventeen-year-old. This is epitomized by the Christmas gifts I got this year. In addition to the usual teenage girl stuff (a Katy Perry CD, jewelry, really cute mittens), I also got a stainless steel skillet, a square griddle, a ten-speed hand mixer, a baking spatula, and rubber prep bowls. And they thrilled me to no end. As you can tell, I love to cook.

Sitting here now, I smile as I think about the day before that Christmas. On that Christmas Eve, I spent hours in the kitchen, up to my elbows in flour and sugar. I scooped peanut-butter cookie dough onto baking sheets, then popped a Hershey's Kiss in their center right when they came out of the oven. I used a wooden spoon to roll out the sugar cookie dough I had prepped the night before and cut out cute little snowmen and stars, before rubbing them with egg wash and sprinkles and placing them in the oven. Later that night, I sautéed a handful of chopped onion in butter before adding spinach, artichokes, and cheese to the pan to make the most delicious dip ever. I loved every second in that kitchen, my nose filling with warm aromas and my ears attuned to the sizzle of vegetables. Cooking is pure bliss.

A little more than a year ago, I would never have said that cooking was anything other than a danger to be avoided. But I have grown a lot since then.

You see, after Christmas when I was fifteen, I made a New Year's resolution to lose weight. It started out innocently enough. I cut out chocolate

It started out innocently enough.

milk and juice in favor of water, and scaled down my portions. I already loved running and was a member of a gym, but I kicked my workouts up a notch. I began to lose weight slowly but steadily. I was pleased with the results but wanted my ideal body to come more rapidly.

I should have seen that coming. I am, and probably always will be, a perfectionist. I do not like to settle for being in the middle or doing "well." To be the best, the brightest, the fastest, and now, the skinniest — I jump into projects full force to obtain my goal.

Calories became my obsession. The calories I ate, the calories I burned. It seemed logical to me that I should attempt to burn off every calorie I ate. So I stuck to a strict 1200-calorie-a-day diet (which in reality amounted to probably less than

1000), and burned over 800 calories a day in cardio. I hoped the remaining 400 would be burned from forty-five minutes of full-body strength training.

I panicked if my diet changed even a little. I remember one time when my mother, trying to coax me into being less anxious about food, made me a baked potato with grilled chicken and steamed broccoli. I could not finish it. How was I supposed to know how many calories were in it? Most of my diet was centered on frozen meals and packaged foods that had very precise serving sizes and calories. This plate of food was sheer madness!

Oddly enough, it was during this time that I began to watch cooking shows. My thought was if I could not enjoy the taste of food, at least I could enjoy the sight of it. So Rachael Ray, Giada De Laurentiis, and Bobby Flay became my regular viewing buddies.

I really think I can attribute a good portion of my recovery to those cooking shows. The hosts had such a light and passion in their eyes when they talked about this meat they were searing, or how wonderful the crusty bread would taste when spread with this tangy sauce. Rachael Ray was particularly influential. She was always smiling! I'll never forget something she said on one episode — with great sincerity, she insisted to the camera: "Food should be fun!"

Wait a second. How could food be fun? Food made you fat. Food was very scary.

> I can attribute a good portion of my recovery to those cooking shows.

But gradually, that message began to sink in. Maybe my thoughts about food were skewed.

Other factors played into this realization as well. I was called down to the nurse because my teachers were worried about my rapid weight loss. I got into fights with my mother over the state of my body. I began to have panic attacks when I could not go to the gym. My best friend showed me a text conversation she had had with another one of my friends about how I looked like a skeleton.

Then, slowly but steadily, I began to catch on. I realized that I was hurting my body. I had no period, I had trouble sleeping and, worst of all, I was causing my family and friends anxiety. It took some time, a lot of support from my loved ones, and therapy, but I finally accepted the idea that I needed to gain back some weight.

I also began to put some techniques I learned from my cooking shows into practice. Not necessarily cooking techniques at first, but how the hosts savored and appreciated the food in front of them. Enjoying every bite, appreciating a food's texture and taste, really brought home the idea that food was a good thing. Then I could put the actual cooking techniques into practice.

For what I believe is the first time in my life, I have achieved a healthy balance. I still love to run and work out, but now, if I have a very active day, I know I need to eat more. I eat very healthily, but I do not count calories as much. I recognize that I need to put nutritious food into my body, but I also know that the occasional pizza and the more-than-occasional piece of chocolate will not hurt me.

Now, I am hungry. I think I will make an egg white frittata with any vegetables I can find, and serve it alongside a freshly sliced tomato and a healthy scoop of salsa. Yum!

—Fallon Kane—
Chicken Soup for the Soul: Just for Teenagers

Redefining Limitations

Life shrinks or expands in
proportion to one's courage.
~Anaïs Nin

I sat in the guidance counselor's office my senior year of high school, bright eyed about the possibilities of college. The counselor sighed and pushed her glasses onto her head. "Are you sure you want to go to college?" she asked. "It will be difficult with your limitations, you know." My limitation, as she called it, was diabetes. I was in three AP classes, a varsity athlete on the track and field team, and nationally ranked in Speech and Debate. But according to her, I was limited.

"Well," I hesitated, unsure of how to respond to her question. Was I sure? Yes, I was absolutely sure that I wanted to go to college. But I started to feel a gnawing monster in my belly, questioning my ability to succeed. Later that night at home, I helped my mom fold laundry in the living room. "What would you think if I just went to community college for a while and figured it out?" I asked her.

> I was glad my mom was by my side for this battle, because I had a feeling it would turn into full-on war.

She looked at me, confused. My mother had left school to start a family. "What do you mean, figure it out?" I told her about my meeting with the guidance counselor, and watched her face change from confusion to anger. I was glad my mom was by my side for this battle, because I had a feeling it would turn into full-on war.

I talked to the admissions counselor at the school I really wanted to go to. All I was missing was my official high school transcript. I promised to have it in the mail the next day, and took a stamped envelope with my forms to the guidance office. Two weeks later, I received a rejection letter, and I called the admissions counselor in tears. "You promised!" I sobbed into the phone, disconsolate about what I perceived to be my dream school. Soothing me over the phone, she pulled up my file, and told me that they never received my official transcript. I never saw anger in color until that afternoon. I called my high school and demanded answers. I sat for hours in the guidance suite, and brought a ferocious mama bear with me. We couldn't prove anything, and my counselor's simpering smile totally and utterly defeated me.

I was burning. I knew that I could not lie down and accept defeat because then my "limitation" would win. I revamped my college efforts, and eventually accepted a track scholarship to Cabrini College, where I spent four magnificent years growing into a woman that I can be proud of. After the track team was cut for budgetary reasons, I focused on social justice, a specialty of Cabrini. I had started insulin pump therapy my freshman year, which gave me an entirely new outlook on living with diabetes. I was able to throw myself into the service of others.

During January of my senior year, I went on a life-changing mission trip called Rostro de Cristo to a small town called Durán in Ecuador. The week I spent there with my classmates and the wonderful residents of that town created memories that I will never forget. The people, the places, the food — they all hold a special place in my heart.

> The devastation of what she did to me propelled me to do my best and pursue my passions.

As I sat on the concrete ground of a schoolyard in Ecuador that week, with a child on each knee, I thought about how lucky I was to have had that guidance counselor in my life. The devastation of what she did to me propelled me to do my best and pursue my passions. As José fingered the tubing coming out of my pocket, I gently explained to him in broken Spanish that it was for my diabetes. He hugged me tightly, taking my breath away, and stood at the gate each day to hug me as we came into the school.

That mission trip lit a fire in me for helping others, and when I got back to the States, I filled out applications for yearlong service opportunities. I graduated in 2012 with two bachelor degrees and my teaching certification, along with high honors and accolades from the honors college. I was accepted by the Mercy Volunteer Corps and went to serve at the Navajo Nation Indian Reservation in rural Arizona. I spent the year after graduation teaching high school U.S. Government and Psychology, and working as a part-time secretary. Now, I am in grad school full-time and working in a high school in North Philadelphia as I study to become a reading specialist.

I still have diabetes, and unless there is a breakthrough, I will always have diabetes. What I don't have are limitations. My ability to serve others and to teach — that's something diabetes cannot take away from me. They are something an out-of-touch counselor cannot take away from me. My biggest "limitation" was not my endocrine system, but my inability to believe in myself. Once I overcame that fear, I realized nothing could stop me from reaching for the stars.

From the streets of Ecuador, to the hogans of the Navajo Nation, to my cluttered classroom in Philadelphia, nothing can limit me. Have insulin pump, will travel.

— Jamie Tadrzynski —
Chicken Soup for the Soul: Find Your Inner Strength

The Academic Jock

I know not what the future holds, but I
know who holds the future.
~Author Unknown

I hate crutches. They slow you to a snail's pace and make your armpits ache. In elementary school, I always wanted to be on crutches, because they got special attention from all the teachers and looked really cool. Once I was actually on crutches, my body ached all over and my dreams of playing on the high school soccer team had been completely crushed. It was my sophomore year of high school, my last chance to at least be a benchwarmer, since all the starters would be the girls who played on the freshman team. The previous year I hadn't even had a chance to try out for soccer — tryouts started right after I busted my knee for the first time.

To say I'm a stubborn and willful person would be an understatement. After I first landed on crutches, I returned to the soccer field in two weeks, and within two minutes of the first half I dislocated the same knee. However, I wasn't deterred just yet. I harbored the hope that if I rested my knee for the remainder of the year, I would be able to try out for the high school JV soccer team the next fall. So I waited patiently and even finished a good season without injury. My optimism was high. Tryouts for the JV team started off with a bang, and the coach noticed me enough to use me as a demonstrator in some of the drills.

> **Within two minutes of the first half I dislocated the same knee.**

Then it happened. On the fourth day of tryouts, we were doing a simple passing drill when my turn came and I made my pass. I quickly turned around, pivoting on my twice-injured knee to return to the line — big mistake. My breath caught in my throat and my left leg went numb as my knee quickly popped abnormally. It was so quick that no one noticed. I was able to hobble my way through the rest of the tryout. The next day, I made an emergency doctor's appointment to make sure I could continue with tryouts. It turned out I couldn't — I was done. The towel had been thrown in for me.

Tryouts weren't over yet, but I knew what I had to do. I slowly made my way on my crutches to the coach's room and explained my situation; I wasn't going to be able to finish tryouts. He was nice enough about it. He told me he was sorry and thought I would've been a great asset to the team. Of course, I didn't want to hear that last part — now that I knew I would've made the team, I was in an even darker mood. What did I have now? Soccer was my pride, my core. Now I had nothing — no real future other than graduating high school, since I still wasn't sure if I wanted to go to college.

I hobbled my way to my English class and scribbled in the last couple of paragraphs to an essay that was due that morning. I was one of the few people who turned in handwritten essays, but it was the easiest way to do it and I didn't care.

> **Now I had nothing—no real future.**

"Ms. Bermudez, your essay please," snapped my English teacher. I ignored him as I wrote my last sentence and quickly held it up to his crossed arms.

"Sorry." I gave a weak smile, but I was in no mood to make up an excuse. He gave me one last glare and continued with the rest of his lecture. Just what I need, I thought. Someone else who thinks I'm a failure. The rest of the week passed in a blur and I spent the weekend sulking in bed, my knee iced and propped up.

Then Monday rolled around and I had a pleasant surprise waiting for me on my desk in English: an A- on the paper I had written partially in class the day it was due.

However, my triumph was short-lived. Before class ended, my English teacher told me I had to stay and talk to him after everyone left. I sulked in anticipation of the lecture I was about to receive. Couldn't he see I was on crutches? Give me a break! It took me almost ten minutes to get from class to class.

"Ms. Bermudez, have you ever heard of the Academic Decathlon?" he started.

"No, I haven't. Why?" I asked suspiciously.

"Basically it's a competition with other schools in ten

different academic tests including speech, interview, essay, literature, etc. I think you would be a great asset to our team. I'm one of the coaches and we meet twice a week after school. We expect you to study on your own in the meantime." He must have caught the face I made at the thought of taking tests and studying for fun, so he continued, "Ms. Bermudez, your half-ass work always gets you an A. You think quickly on your feet and you retain information like a sponge. I have a feeling you'd definitely place and win some medals in a few of the subject areas."

I laughed at his "half-ass" comment and said I'd give it a shot. Might as well. What else was I going to do with myself? Plus, it would be pretty cool to win some awards for the school, and it would look great on college apps if I decided on that route.

I can't lie and say that I didn't have fun over the three months of prep work before the competition. The team was an eclectic group of students because, as it turned out, the competition required students with all levels of GPAs — 2.0, 3.0, 4.0. I was in the 3.0 group and carried my weight easily.

The day of the competition we were up against six other schools in our region. It was an all day event and my parents even showed up for the Super Quiz, which required students to sit on stage and answer questions in open competition. I couldn't help but smile as I heard my Dad cheer us on from the audience. It really was exciting.

I went home with three medals — two for second place in speech and first place in super quiz with the rest of the team.

> **It turns out that when I lost the chance to play soccer, I found a new future for myself.**

Who knew academics could be so rewarding? I had a gift for learning that I had never realized before, and now I was ready to exploit it. My time as a jock was over — not that I couldn't enjoy the occasional recreational sport — but I knew my future now revolved around academics, honors classes, AP courses, and eventually college. It turns out that when I lost the chance to play soccer, I found a new future for myself.

— Tanya Bermudez —
Chicken Soup for the Soul: Teens Talk High School

Choices

Drinking and driving: there are stupider
things, but it's a very short list.
—Author Unknown

I grew up in a small town outside Savannah, Georgia where no one locked their doors at night and the main entertainment was Friday night high school football. The only crime to speak of was the occasional speeding ticket and maybe every once in a while a fight would break out at the one and only bar in town on a Saturday night. It's just a sleepy little town where parents want to raise their children away from the crime and danger of a big city, and where teenagers dream of leaving to find something bigger and better.

All that changed for me on one muggy summer night in July. It was my eighteenth birthday. My best friend Lisa's parents were going to be out of town for the week, so Lisa and my other two best friends, Kim and Jewel, decided to throw me a party at Lisa's house. My parents thought I was going out to dinner with Tyler, my boyfriend, then going over to Kim's to stay the rest of the weekend. Tyler came by to pick me up at six. My parents always said the same thing to Tyler before every date: "Drive carefully. You are driving around with precious cargo in your passenger seat." My mom gave us hugs and sent us out the door.

When Tyler and I arrived at Lisa's, the party was already in full swing—Lisa's house was packed. We had always liked going to parties and hanging out with our friends, although neither of us drank alcohol or did drugs. However, a few days before, Tyler and I had decided to maybe have a few drinks at the party. As soon as Kim and Jewel found out I was drinking, they both joined in. After about three margaritas and some other random drinks people just kept handing to me, I was pretty drunk, so I quit to look for Tyler. By the time I found Tyler, I was feeling sick and I wanted to go home. But we had a problem: Tyler was just as drunk as I was, if not more. When I told Tyler I needed to go home because I wasn't feeling good, he said he was fine and he'd take me home. Even as drunk as I was I still knew better, we both knew better then to drink and drive. At that point I just didn't care—all I could think of was how much I wanted to go home.

With some difficulty, Tyler and I made it out to his car. I don't remember getting home or much after, for that matter. I do remember my parents running outside in their pajamas and how scared they both looked. My mom helped me to my

> Tyler and I had decided to maybe have a few drinks at the party.

bed and my dad put Tyler to bed on the couch.

That night, after puking up my guts, I finally fell asleep and had a bad dream:

It's early morning. I wake up to my parents crying. Kim, my friend since we were five years old, has been killed in a car accident. After Tyler and I left, Kim, who had more to drink than me, got into her car. She didn't put her seatbelt on, didn't turn her headlights on, and headed towards the highway to go home. She was going about ninety miles per hour and driving on the wrong side of the road. Kim never saw the truck coming. The driver, who also wasn't wearing a seatbelt, didn't see her in time to swerve. They hit head on. Kim died immediately, and the driver was thrown through the truck windshield and was in a coma.

I woke in the late afternoon, screaming out Kim's name in a cold sweat with tears running down my face. My mother rushed into my room and held me until I stopped crying.

It's been eleven years since that night, and I haven't touched alcohol again. Every year around my birthday I have the same nightmare over and over again. I see my parents crying while they come into my room to tell me what happened to Kim. The only difference is that now my mother isn't around to hold me until the tears stop and tell me it really is a nightmare, not just the alcohol fogging my brain. Because Kim really did hit that truck. I later learned the driver's name was David, and he was in a coma for a week before he died. He left behind a three-year-old son, who was named after him, and a wife seven months pregnant with a little girl.

Whenever I look back on that day, I wonder if Kim would have been drinking if I hadn't. I wonder if she would have driven home if she hadn't seen me do it first. What would have happened if I hadn't made the choice to drink that night? Would Kim still be alive? Would David? I know Kim made the choice to drink and drive that night, but a part of me will always feel responsible for what happened.

> Every choice, whether good or bad, is like a pebble dropped into still water.

I may not have changed the world with my story, but I do hope that by sharing it I make people realize the responsibility they have to themselves and to everyone else out there. Don't ever think that your choices are yours alone. Every choice, whether good or bad, is like a pebble dropped into still water — each ripple represents someone your choice affects. That's quite an impact, isn't it?

— Makaila Fenwick —
Chicken Soup for the Soul: Tough Times for Teens

MEET OUR CONTRIBUTORS

We are pleased to introduce you to the writers whose stories were compiled from our past books to create this new collection. These bios were the ones that ran when the stories were originally published. They were current as of the publication dates of those books.

Devora Adams is a writer and life coach who lives in New Jersey with her husband and four daughters. She is the author of *Amazing Women: Jewish Voices of Inspiration*, published by Menucha Publishers, as well as a proud contributor to the *Chicken Soup for the Soul* series. E-mail her at the_write_direction@yahoo.com.

Brittany Autumn Austin is a passionate advocate for individuals with autism. She volunteered in a self-contained classroom for six years in high school and went on to major in Special Education, with honors. She is driven by her hopes, dreams, and family. E-mail Brittany at Baustin@mail.niagara.edu.

Fifteen-year-old **Adam Avin** created Wuf Shanti to teach mindfulness so kids can live in health, wellness, peace and positivity and to help them cope with emotions, stress and to interact with kindness. He founded the Kids' Association for Mindfulness in Education, and the Mindful Kids Peace Summit. Adam gave a TEDxYouthTalk about mindfulness.

Tanya Bermudez graduated from UC Davis with two B.A.'s in Economics and International Relations and will graduate in 2010 with her MBA. She works in Sacramento, CA for an educational advocacy firm and is passionate about travel, reading, writing, and being active in the Sacramento community. E-mail her at bermudez.tanya@gmail.com.

Louis R. Cardona lives in Chicago, IL. He is currently taking classes in graphic design. He enjoys shooting pool, writing, reading, and baseball. He is artistic and creative. He wrote this story when he was still in high school, and hopes to do more writing in the future.

Savannah D. Cassel is a registered nurse living in Central Pennsylvania. She is honored to be publishing her second story in the *Chicken Soup for the Soul* series and is married to the man that inspired her first story featured in *Chicken Soup for the Soul: The Power of Gratitude*.

Madeline Clapps lives in Brooklyn with her boyfriend and her cat Vanilla Bean. She went to New York University and is a singer, writer, and editor, with many stories published in *Chicken Soup for the Soul* books.

Amber Curtis is a junior at Western Wayne. She enjoys running and writing. She credits her success to Mr. Rebar and

Mr. Usher. She resides with her parents and sister by their grandparents' dairy farm. Please e-mail her at talkativeamber@yahoo.com.

Brie Dalliant has since overcome her depression. She wishes for everyone out there to know that one life can change the world. One life can make a difference, and you are one life. Though she hopes to pursue a medical career when she is older, she plans on writing as a side job or hobby.

Christine Dixon is a freelance writer, and is currently studying book publishing at Ryerson University. She currently writes a food and drink column for *Cottage Magazine* in Canada. E-mail her at vangoach@bmts.com.

Patricia Dublin received her Bachelor of Nursing and Associate of Arts, with honors, from Austin Peay State University. She has four daughters and is married to her loving and supportive husband Sergeant Troy Dublin. She enjoys cruising and writing, and this is the first story she has ever submitted to be published.

Makaila Fenwick lives in the little town of Willis in the big state of Texas where she and her husband Chris are raising their two-year-old daughter. Makaila volunteers in youth ministry at their church and loves it.

Michael Ford lives in Florida and is obtaining a bachelor's degree in Psychology. He plans on moving to California and becoming a teacher or guidance counselor.

Derek H. is the author of several novels and a collection of short stories. His books are widely read and are available online.

Deanne Haines is a Wisconsin-based freelance writer and frequent contributor to parenting magazines across the country. She feels blessed to have a wonderful husband, three children and amazing friends — old and new. In her spare time Deanne enjoys running and traveling to exciting locales. Find out more at DeanneHaines.com.

David Hull lives in the small upstate New York town of Holley, where he enjoys reading, writing, gardening and spoiling his nieces and nephews. He is a retired teacher.

Miranda Johnson is currently in high school and will graduate in 2014. She is involved in marching band and plays piano, flute, is learning alto sax, and is also interested in art.

Fallon Kane is a twenty-year-old student currently studying psychology and criminal justice at Adelphi University. This is her fourth story published in the *Chicken Soup for the Soul* series. Other than writing, Fallon enjoys food, running, and research. She would like to thank the Murwins at Awesome Country for inspiring this story!

Kathleen Kohler writes about the ups and downs of family life for numerous magazines and anthologies. She and her husband live in the Pacific Northwest, and have three children and seven grandchildren. Visit www.kathleenkohler. com to read more of her articles or enter her latest contest.

Madison Kurth is a senior in high school. She plays varsity soccer and wrestles for her school. Madison has a strong fascination with biology and hopes to have a career in the medical field.

Mallory Lavoie received her Bachelor of Arts degree from the University of Maine in 2012. She lives in Maine, where she works as a marketer and figure skating coach. She enjoys running, reading, playing the piano, and spending time with her dog, Mowgli.

Victoria Linhares is a seventeen-year-old high school student and aspiring writer. She enjoys traveling, art, and literature. Her favourite book is *Extremely Loud and Incredibly Close* by Jonathan Safran Foer. E-mail her at victorialinhares@ymail.com.

Pittsburgh native **Kelly Starling Lyons** is the author of picture book, *One Million Men and Me*, and chapter book, *NEATE: Eddie's Ordeal*. She has two forthcoming picture books with G.P. Putnam's Sons. Kelly lives in North Carolina and leads a book club for girls. Visit Kelly at www.kellystarlinglyons.com.

Aimee McCarron is currently a sophomore at the University of Massachusetts at Lowell. She lives with her family in Burlington, Massachusetts. Aimee enjoys reading, traveling, watching movies, and baking.

Christopher McDaniel is currently a dancer with the Los Angeles Ballet. He is simultaneously on the faculty at Lula Washington Dance Theatre. During his off time he enjoys going to the beach, going out dancing with friends, and seeing other forms of art. E-mail him at chrismcdaniel08@gmail.com.

Brianna Mears is a high school student from Austin, TX. She feels the most herself on the court with her tennis team and enjoys spending time with friends. Brianna has always enjoyed her academic courses, but has recently discovered her passion for English and writing.

Like most people who tell their story about singing from the day they were born, **Samantha Molinaro's** passion for writing was seeded at birth. The bottom line remains that for Samantha, writing is an escape and mode of expression in which she hopes others can be inspired to laugh, cry, or even write themselves.

Brianne Monett-Curran is currently pursuing a Bachelor of Science degree, in Seattle, WA, where she lives with her husband. She enjoys camping, traveling and a good cup of coffee.

Kaitlin Murray loves to travel, write, and volunteer. She was born in Holland and has also lived in Germany, France, the USA, and Italy. For the past two years, Kaitlin has been traveling full-time and volunteering all over the world. She also founded a charity called Kids Unite 4 Hope to help children in need. Read her blog at travelinkait.com.

Annie Nason is currently a junior in college. She has been a guest blogger for Teen Cerebral Palsy at TeenCerebralPalsy. com since 2012. "Three Simple Words" is her first published piece, and truly a dream come true! Annie would like to thank her family and friends for all their support and encouragement. She is incredibly grateful for this opportunity!

Faith Northmen received her Bachelor of Arts, with honors, concentration in Medieval Literature, and Master's degree from the University of California, Irvine. Faith teaches high school English and actively studies history and science-fiction/fantasy. E-mail her at englishgoverness@yahoo.com.

Heidi Patton is an aspiring journalist. She writes for her school newspaper and plans to continue writing at the University of San Francisco. She loves traveling, running, volunteering, and the Oregon coast. She once won a contest for the best fifty-five-word short story. E-mail at heidipatton6@hotmail.com.

Lisa Solorzano Petit received her Bachelor of Science in Rehabilitation Services from the University of Maine at Farmington in 2005. She loves her family and loves being a stay-at-home mom to her two boys. Lisa is excited to realize a dream in seeing her work published! She enjoys living life to its fullest.

Lydia Gomez Reyes is a published writer and poet. Her love for God is the driving force behind her writing. Several of her devotionals and poems have appeared in *The Secret Place*. Lydia lives in Colorado Springs, CO with her husband, Rey, of thirty-five years. Learn more at www.lydiareyes.com.

Tracy Rusiniak showed her father, Stephen, a frequent Chicken Soup for the Soul contributor, her college entrance essay about a church mission trip to Appalachia. Together they crafted her submission into the story found in this book. Now a college graduate, Tracy, originally from New Jersey, is currently living in Hawaii.

Diane Stark is a former teacher turned stay-at-home mom and freelance writer. She is a frequent contributor to the *Chicken Soup for the Soul* series, and she loves to write about the important things in life: her family and her faith. E-mail her at DianeStark19@yahoo.com.

Alexis Streb was born in 1997 and has always been a Navy brat. She has been all over the world, from Guam, to D.C. and back again. Alexis is a homeschooled vegetarian who reads and plays soccer all the time. E-mail her at alexis.streb@hotmail.com.

Jamie Tadrzynski received her master's degree in May of 2015 as part of the Alliance for Catholic Education at Saint Joseph's University. Prior to grad school, she served as a yearlong volunteer teacher at Saint Michael Indian School on the Navajo Nation in Arizona. Read more at www.joysandsorrowsmingled. blogspot.com.

Rajkumar Thangavelu graduated from Bucknell University with a B.A. degree in Economics and Political Science in 1998. He currently works for the federal government in Washington, D.C. He loves to travel and enjoys volunteering with children. E-mail him at rajkt@hotmail.com.

Megan Thurlow studies at Kansas State University, and is a member of the Pi Beta Phi fraternity for women. She enjoys reading, singing, acting and playing sports in her free time. Megan's future plans are undecided. E-mail her at mthurlow@ k-state.edu.

McKenzie Vaught is currently enrolled at Somerset Community College and plans to go to Eastern Kentucky University to complete her degree in psychology. Her mother gets out of prison in September of 2014.

Nicole Webster has been interested in writing since the age of eight. She has self-published a children's book with her sister, titled *Sleepingcinderpunzlewhite*, available on blurb. com. Her other interests include reading, scrapbooking and cooking. She currently resides in Utah with her husband and four children.

Christy Westbrook completed a BAIS in Early Childhood Education and a Master of Library and Information Science from the University of South Carolina. She lives in Lexington, South Carolina with her husband, Thad, and their two daughters, Abby and Katie.

Juliette Rose Wunrow is currently a high school student. Prior to moving to the United States she and her family lived in the Fiji Islands and New Zealand. After high school, she plans to attend college in the New England area. Her interests include writing, art, French, and running.

MEET
AMY NEWMARK

Amy Newmark is the bestselling author, editor-in-chief, and publisher of the *Chicken Soup for the Soul* book series. Since 2008, she has published 165 new books, most of them national bestsellers in the U.S. and Canada, more than doubling the number of Chicken Soup for the Soul titles in print today. She is also the author of *Simply Happy*, a crash course in Chicken Soup for the Soul advice and wisdom that is filled with easy-to-implement, practical tips for enjoying a better life.

Amy is credited with revitalizing the Chicken Soup for the Soul brand, which has been a publishing industry phenomenon since the first book came out in 1993. By compiling inspirational and aspirational true stories curated from ordinary people who have had extraordinary experiences, Amy has kept the twenty-seven-year-old Chicken Soup for the Soul brand fresh and relevant.

Amy graduated *magna cum laude* from Harvard University where she majored in Portuguese and minored in French. She then embarked on a three-decade career as a Wall Street analyst, a hedge fund manager, and a corporate executive in the technology field. She is a Chartered Financial Analyst.

Her return to literary pursuits was inevitable, as her honors thesis in college involved traveling throughout Brazil's impoverished northeast region, collecting stories from regular people. She is delighted to have come full circle in her writing career — from collecting stories "from the people" in Brazil as a twenty-year-old to, three decades later, collecting stories "from the people" for Chicken Soup for the Soul.

When Amy and her husband Bill, the CEO of Chicken Soup for the Soul, are not working, they are visiting their four grown children and their grandchildren.

Follow Amy on Twitter @amynewmark. Listen to her free podcast — "Chicken Soup for the Soul with Amy Newmark" — on Apple Podcasts, Google Play, the Podcasts app on iPhone, or by using your favorite podcast app on other devices.

Changing the world one story at a time®
www.chickensoup.com